Hobbyist Guide
—— To ——
Successful Pond Keeping

Dr. David Pool

ACKNOWLEDGEMENTS

I would like to thank Maureen Beart, Georg Grützner
and Jackie Pool for their invaluable help in the
preparation of this book.

© 1993
Tetra-Press
Tetra-Werke Dr. rer nat. Ulrich Baensch GmbH
P.O. Box 1580. D-49 304 Melle, Germany
All right reserved, incl. film, broadcasting,
television as well as the reprinting
1st edition 1-10.000, 1993
Printed in Germany by Busse Druck
DLB - 30.313-93

Distributed in the U.S.A. by
Tetra Sales U.S.A.,
3001 Commerce Street
Blacksburg, VA 24060

Distributed in UK by
Tetra Sales, Lambert Court,
Chestnut Avenue, Eastleigh, Hampshire S05 3ZQ
WL-Code: 16584

ISBN 3-89356-135-8

Contents

Introduction

Coldwater fishkeeping in general and pondkeeping in particular is now enjoying a boom in popularity, with more and more people installing ponds in their gardens.

The reasons for building a pond vary considerably. For some it is an extension to the garden and few if any fish are added. For others the reverse is true, with the pond being devoted exclusively to the fish. Similarly the size, shape and complexity of the pond vary greatly depending on individuals taste and the area available. Whatever the size, shape or occupants, there is no doubt that a well maintained pond enhances the appearance of any garden and quickly becomes the centre of attention.

In this hobbyist guide we examine the ways of setting up and maintaining a pond in peak condition. Constructing a pond was, until recently, a complicated process involving the use of precast ponds or concrete. With the advent of butyl liners, however, the process is very much easier and can be accomplished by any fishkeeper or gardener. In the first article the basic steps involved in constructing such a pond are described. The importance of planning your pond and it surroundings

cannot be overstressed. Looking at other ponds and talking with their owners is a useful way of ensuring that you avoid many of the pitfalls and end up with the type of pond that you had envisaged.

Other chapters concentrate on caring for your pond and selecting the plants and fish to stock it with. Once established the pond should require a minimum of maintenance to keep it looking at its best. It is in the early stages that problems can occur, particularly when selecting and introducing the living components. It is always advisable to select a high class aquarist dealer or garden centre from which to purchase your plants and fish. In addition to healthy disease free stock, such a dealer will also be able to provide invaluable advice on all aspects of pondkeeping.

There is little doubt that, once installed, your pond will become the centre of attraction, not only for yourselves, but also for innumerable forms of wildlife, ranging from dragonflies to water birds. It is hardly surprising, therefore, that pondkeeping is becoming so popular.

Dr. David Pool

A Well Planted Natural Pond. Photo: Tetra

GARDEN POND CONSTRUCTION

Most gardens benefit from the addition of a garden pond. The presence of an area of water, together with colourful fish and plants not only provides a great deal of interest, but also acts as a focal point for the garden and provides an ideal setting for relaxation on a summer afternoon or evening.

The rewards of such a pool will far outweigh the small expense and effort involved in its creation and upkeep.

Planning the pond

The first stage in the construction of a pond should be to carefully plan where the pond is to be sited and what design is required. Visiting local water garden centres and friends or acquaintances who have ponds is an ideal way to see the range of ponds available as well as being able to discuss the advantages and disadvantages of each pond. Time spent at this stage of construction is not wasted and will result in you choosing the correct pond for your garden and reduce the occurrence of future problems.

Siting the pond

A number of points need to be considered when selecting a site for your pond:

a) Sunlight is important to ensure healthy plant growth, but in excess will cause algae problems. Therefore select a site where the pond will receive at least half a days sunlight, but get some shade from the bright afternoon sun.

Your pond will attract a great deal of interest, so position it where it can be seen from a window or patio. Photo: PIAG

Careful use of a bridge enhances the appearance of a pond - and is easy to construct and install. Photo: Sakanaya

b) Trees can also pose problems due to their roots growing under the pond and the leaves falling in and polluting the water, so choose a site away from overhanging trees.

c) The pond will be the centre of attraction in the garden, so position it where it can be easily viewed from, say, a terrace, patio or window.

Pond design

The design of your garden pond will largely depend upon personal preferences, although it will also be influenced by the size of the garden and fish you wish to keep. Ponds for koi, for example, are usually deeper than a normal pond, have no plants and have a large external filter. The following points should be considered when designing your pond:

a) Wherever possible the pond should be at least 30 square feet (3 m²) with a depth of 18 inches (45 cm) or greater. Ponds of this size tend to be more easy to care for and are more likely to attain a balance between the fish and plants resulting in clear water. The depth of the water is particularly important in cool climates where ice can form on the water surface.

If you live in an area which experiences very cold winters it is advisable to make the pond 30 inches (75 cm) deep.

A pond will be add beauty to any garden Photo: K-H. Wieser

b) The profile of the pond can be varied to suit individual tastes. If marginal plants are to be added a shelf 9 inches (23 cm) below water level and 9 inches wide should be included. This will accommodate a 6 inch (15 cm) deep planting container giving a shallow depth of water above it's surface.

The sides of the pond should not slope too steeply as they may become less stable and be adversely affected by ice forma-tion. An angle of 60° to the horizontal (or less) is ideal.

c) Safety is particularly important since the pond will have a magical attraction for children. Building a raised pond or constructing a fence around the pond will reduce access to children. Alternatively you can design the pond so that it is difficult for a child to get to the deeper, and more dangerous water. The area surrounding the deep water should be laid out as a shallow zone, ½ to 2

Above: Japanese Style Gardens are landscaped with large rocks and carefully sited plants. Photo: Sakanaya

Left:With a little thought and ingenuity a pond can be constructed on a slope. Photo: Tetra

feet (45-60 cm) wide and 4-8 inches (10-20 cm) deep. This can be landscaped with large stones, boulders and bogwood together with tall marginal plants to create a natural barrier to an inquisitive child.

d) Soil removed from the pond excavation can be used to form a rockery around the pond or as the basis for a waterfall.

Construction

There are three methods of garden pond construction: concrete, purchasing a fibre glass preformed pond and construction utilizing a flexible pond liner. The latter is by far the best choice in terms of price, ease of installation, durability and flexibility of design. These pond lin-

ers are available in different material grades ranging from very cheap, thin plastic to heavy duty rubber liners. As with most items, you should seek out quality and reliability of manufacture and relegate price to a secondary consideration.

The size of liner needed for a particular pond can be calculated in the following way. Length of liner = length of pond + twice the maximum depth, and width of liner = width of pond + twice the maximum depth. For example for an 8 feet x 6 feet pond, with a maximum depth of 2 feet, the liner would be 8 feet + (2 x 2 feet) = 12 feet long and 6 feet + (2 x 2 feet) = 10 feet wide. Construction of the pond can be undertaken at any time, but is best conducted during the spring and

13

A small waterfall will add character to the pond. Photo: K-H. Wieser

early summer. At this time of the year the ground will not be frozen or waterlogged, and once finished the pond plus its inhabitants will have time to become established before the rigours of winter. The construction of a liner pond can be divided into a number of stages, and these are shown in the following sequence of photographs.

STAGE 1: A hosepipe, rope or series of wooden pegs should be laid out in the required pond shape. When final adjustments to the shape have been made digging can commence. Always start slightly inside the final outline to allow for final shaping. The first stage of excavation is to remove the turf, if the pond is sited on a lawn, or to remove the soil down to a depth of 6 inches (15 cm).

Hobbyist Guide
To
Successful Pond Keeping

STAGE 2: Start digging at the pools projected deepest point and gradually work outwards. The deepwater area and position of any shelves may be marked using pegs, hosepipe or rope to enable you to follow the original plan more closely. Once the deep area of the pond has been excavated marginal shelves can be constructed in the sides.

STAGE 3: Regular checks of the depths are necessary to ensure that you follow your plans. Undisturbed soil makes a much better foundation for the pond than an area that has been backfilled and firmed. Checks should also be made using a spirit level to ensure that the top edge of the pond is level, since the water will immediately show any faults.

STAGE 4: After final trimming and shaping, the side and base of the excavation must be closely inspected using bare hands and any sharp stones or roots removed.
A layer of sand approximately ½ inch (1.5 cm) deep should be used to line the excavation and produce a smooth surface which will not damage the liner. On stony ground, polyester matting or old carpet should also be used as an added precaution.

A Delightful Stone Bridge. Photo: D. Pool

STAGE 5: The pool liner should be draped loosely into the excavation with an even overlap all around. Stones should be positioned at each corner and along the sides to hold the liner in position. As the pond fills, the stones should be lifted occasionally to allow the liner to fit snugly into the excavation. Some creasing is inevitable, but this can be minimised by stretching and manipulating the liner as the pond fills.

STAGE 6: When the pond is full the surplus lining can be cut off, leaving a 6 inch (15 cm) flap around the side. This can be temporarily secured using nails to ensure that the liner does not slip. Ensure that the edge of the liner is cut off and secured above the level of the surrounding ground. This will prevent water draining into the pond from the surrounding garden, or water being syphoned out of the pond by capillary action.

STAGE 7: Formal ponds can be lined with stone slabs. These should be laid out on a bed of mortar comprising 3 parts sand to 1 part cement. The stones should overlap the pond edge by 1-2 inches (2-5 cm) to conceal the liner and protect it from the suns rays.

Once completed the pond should be drained and refilled before fish or plants are added, particularly if cement has fallen into the water during construction.

STAGE 8: Informal ponds can be surrounded with pieces of rock, gravel and bogwood, which can be arranged to provide a natural transition from dry land to the water. Marginal plants can be positioned in the gravel or shallow water to enhance the natural appearance of the pond. With care, the pond can be made to look as though it is not man made!

Photographs courtesy of Stapeley Water Gardens, Nantwich, England.

WATER MOVEMENT IN THE POND

The sight and sound of moving water in your garden adds an extra dimension to pondkeeping and considerably enhances the overall appeal of the pond. However, moving water is not just aesthetic it is also essential to enable the pond to be filtered and to oxygenate the water.

Moving water features are available from any water garden centre or in some cases, can be constructed by enthusiastic pondkeepers. Careful plumbing is important and the following chapter will provide some guidelines to ensure that the water features function effectively.

Choice of Pump

A pump is obviously essential in order to create water movement and power the filter, waterfall, venturi, fountain etc.

The size of pump is determined largely by the size of the pond, the height to which water must be pumped and, to a lesser extent, the type of fish being kept. As a rough guide you should aim to pass the pond water through the filter once every 1-4 hours. In a fish-only, or heavily stocked pond you should aim at once every 1-2 hours, whereas in a well-planted pond the slower turnover rate will be sufficient.

If the filter is positioned well above the pond a more powerful pump will be required to provide the neces-

sary turnover rate. Finally, if Koi are kept you should aim for a slightly faster turnover rate in order to cope with the large amounts of waste produced. Whichever pump you select, it is important to ensure that is safe. Always follow the manufacturer's instructions and use waterproof connections, where required, together with a circuit breaker (which will automatically cut off the power should there be any damage to the pump or cable). The position of the pump in the pond and in relation to the filter, together with the size of the associated pipework is also important if the filter is to operate at its maximum efficiency with minimal maintenance.

A pump is essential for water movement and it is worth purchasing a good quality model. Photo: D. Pool

19

A BOTTOM DRAIN SYSTEM

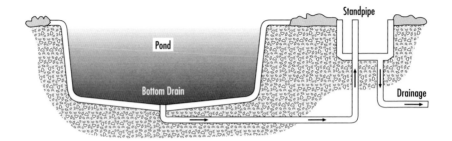

Standpipe

Pond

Bottom Drain

Drainage

PUMP FED

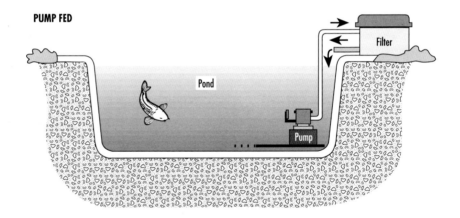

Filter

Pond

Pump

GRAVITY FED

The difference between pump fed (above)
and gravity fed filter systems (below)

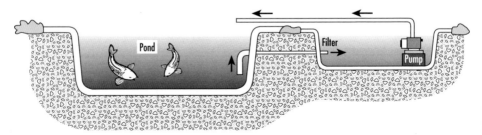

Pond

Filter

Pump

Pipework

The diameter of the pipes used with the pump should be that recommended in its instruction leaflet, which is usually the diameter of the pump outflow. Using a wider diameter pipe will greatly reduce the water pressure and rate of flow, resulting in sediment settling and possibly blocking the pipes.

A narrower pipe will create greater resistance to the water and thus reduce the output of the pump. Bends in the pipework should be kept to a minimum, with sharp bends avoided if at all possible as they will reduce water flow. Finally, the total length of pipework should be kept as short as possible as again the friction in the pipes will reduce the water flow.

Filter and pump positions

The filter itself is usually positioned level with the pond (ie. the water level in each is the same) orr above the water level in the pond.

If the filter is above the pond, water has to be pumped into the filter, but returns to the pond by gravity. These "pump fed" filters are generally used in small or medium sized ponds.

To prevent debris being drawn into the pump some form of pre- filtration is necessary. This may be in the form of a block of coarse foam or even a piece of plastic mesh. To reduce blockage this "pre-filter" should have a large external surface area.

So, for example, a fine plastic mesh stretched over the pump inflow would rapidly block, whereas the same mesh covering a 20 x 20 x 20 cm planting basket placed over the pump inflow would block less frequently.

Larger external filters particularly for Koi ponds, usually have the same water level as the pond. In such filters it is advisable to place the pump after the filter, to pump clean water back into the pond.

Water will then be syphoned into the filter through a pipe positioned at the start of the filter. Such a system is known as a "gravity-fed" filter.

The main advantage of such a system is that the pump is not exposed to dirty water, therefore the risk of blockage is minimal. Also if the pump is switched off for any reason (eg when treating the pond with a remedy which would kill the filter bacteria), the filter will remain filled with water, and the pump can be used to circulate water within filter so reducing bacterial death.

Position of the filter inflow

The position in the pond from where water should be pumped or drawn into the filter is a matter of some debate among experienced pond and Koi keepers. The choice is between taking water from the bottom or mid-water.

If taken from the bottom of the pond, the water will be rich in waste material and organic matter. It is

this material which should be removed from the pond to maintain good water conditions. However if excessive amounts are sucked up it can block the pump and/or the filter media, which will require regular cleaning. The alternative is to take water from just above the pond bottom.

This water will contain fine debris and chemical waste material, but will not have the problematic coarse debris. The coarse material may be removed at regular intervals using a net, syphon or bottom drain (if fitted).

In practice, it is advisable to have the facility to take water from both the bottom and middle of the pond. In the summer the water and debris can be taken from the bottom, unless the pumpor filter blocks regularly, in which case the pump or inflow should be raised a few inches. In the winter, when the water temperature falls below 6°C the water flow at the pond bottom should be negligible to allow the fish to conserve their energy and to prevent the entire pond from cooling down. At low temperatures water from close to the surface should be taken into the filter.

The position of a submerged pump or flexible pipe can easily be adjusted when necessary, for example by the use of bricks. However in a large Koi pond, particularly one which has a "gravity fed" filter, such flexibility should be considered and incorporated at the construction stage.

Even a small waterfall will create the delightful sound of running water.
Photo: K.-H. Wieser

p. 22/23: A waterfall will greatly enhance the appearance of your pond.
Photo: D. Pool

Water movement is particularly important during hot summers when oxygen concentrations in the pond may be low. Photo: W. Stehling

Waterfalls

A waterfall is a popular addition to the garden pond, with the sound of moving water adding a sense of tranquillity to the pool as well as oxygenating the water.

The waterfall is powered by means of a pump, which can either pass water directly to the top of the waterfall or into an external filter which discharges into the fall. The latter option is particularly good as it ensures that the water from the filter is well oxygenated before returning to the pond.

When selecting a pump it is important that it can provide sufficient water at the "head" required. The "head" is the vertical distance between the pond surface and the top of the waterfall. The greater the head, the less water a given pump,

will be able to pass per hour. For example, a given pump model has an output of 600 gallons per hour at a head of 3 feet, 530gph at 5ft, 400gph at 7ft and only 145gph at 10ft.

The quantity of water required for the waterfall depends upon its width. As a guide 300 gallons per hour will give a thin continuous sheet of water approximately 6 inches wide.

A waterfall may be left running throughout the summer, and must be allowed to do so if it is attached to the filter. In the winter the water movement in the pond created by the fall will cause the water to cool rapidly, and will result in the fish utilising their valuable energy supplies simply by swimming against the flow. For this reason the waterfall should not be used when water temperatures are below 6-8°C.

A fountain can be switched on during periods of hot weather to oxygenate the water. Photo: Tetra

Fountains

Most submersible pumps may be used to power a fountain by the simple addition of a fountain kit, which is comprised of a short extension tube and a spray jet. The extension tube is used so that the fountain jet is slightly above the water level, and a jet is added to produce the required spray pattern.

To prevent the jet rapidly becoming blocked with debris it is advisable to position the pump approximately six inches above the pond bottom and fit a fine strainer over the pump inflow. The height of the fountain is determined by the output of the pump used.

The fountain itself need not be used continually. It may be switched on as required, although it is advisable to keep the fountain running during periods of hot still weather. At these times the oxygenating effect of the moving water will be beneficial to the fish. In the winter the fountain should not be used, in order to avoid unnecessary water movement in the pond.

p. 26/27: A waterfall can be constructed in the mound of soil which is removed when the pond is dug. Photo: Tetra

Water features using moving water need not be directly linked to the pond.
Photo: D. Pool

Pond Drainage

Although the pond will rarely require complete draining, it will occasionally be necessary to remove some water along with any excess debris.

The choice of drainage method depends largely on the size and complexity of the pond. In practice there are four methods used with varying degrees of success:

1. Bucket: Using a bucket to empty the pond is not ideal as most of the water has to be removed before the debris on the bottom can be discarded. This method is only feasible on small patio style ponds, or if surface water and scum has to be removed.

2. Syphon: If there is a drain or soakaway close to and lower than the pond, a length of tubing may be used as a syphon to remove the water. The easiest way to start such a syphon is to immerse the tubing (hosepipe) in the pond and allow it to completely fill with water. Keeping one end of the tubing in the pond, place your hand over the other end in order to form a seal. The sealed end of the tube should then be positioned in the drain or soakaway and the seal removed.

Always be wary of the fish in the pond, which have a fatal attraction for the syphon tube. A net placed over the syphon outflow will prevent accidents.

3. Pond Vacuum: When syphoning water from the pond is difficult or impossible, a pond vacuum can be used to remove debris and water. A pond vacuum is comprised of a water pump and length of tubing. The tubing can be used like a household vacuum to suck up the debris on the pond bottom. It is advisable to remove large debris and leaves using a net prior to vacuuming as they can block the tubing.

4. Purge or Bottom Drains: In many koi ponds drains are installed during construction which greatly simplify water and waste removal. These drains are placed in the deepest part of the pond where waste will accumulate. They can be used either to feed the filter or to drain the pond. An indication of how the purge or bottom drains can be installed is shown in the diagram.

Obviously every garden pond is different and the information provided here may not all be of direct relevance. Specific problems relating to your pond or proposed filter, fountain or waterfall may be answered by your local aquatic or water garden centre.

FILTRATION

Maintaining clean and pollutant free water in your pond is important if the fish and plants are to remain healthy and attractive.

In a lightly stocked pond where the plants are growing well, there should be little problem with the water quality. In such a balanced pond any waste products produced by the fish will quickly be decomposed and the resultant chemicals absorbed by the plants.

For most pondkeepers, however, good water conditions are maintained by using a filter. There are a large variety of filters available for pond use, but all work on the same basic principles.

Mechanical Filtration

This is the process by which any particles of debris in the water are removed. Filter media which work mechanically act as a sieve and strain out these particles. Examples of mechanical media include foam and filter brushes. Within the filter the mechanical filter media should be placed before other forms of filtration in order to prevent them becoming clogged by debris.

Biological Filtration

The biological filter media is the site where the helpful bacteria which consume organic waste are encouraged to grow. In order to

Healthy fish and plants together with clear water - the result of a well filtered balanced pond. Photo: Tetra

A multichambered box filter for larger ponds. The first chamber contains filter brushes for mechanical filtration. The next two chambers are filled with plastic tubing for biological filtration.
Photo: D. Pool

all of the waste produced in the pond. It is also important that the filter medium does not easily become blocked, which would prevent the flow of oxygen rich water. Fine gravel or sand, for example, would provide a very large surface area, but, because it restricts the flow of water and easily becomes blocked, oxygen would only reach the surface layers, with the remainder of the media being ineffective. A wide variety of materials can be used for biological filtration, ranging from foam to gravel, hair rollers to plastic tubing. Whichever you choose do not use a great depth of filter medium as only that close to the water inflow will receive sufficient oxygen. As a guide 15-20cm of gravel or 30-60cm of foam or tubing will ensure that all of the filter is functioning effectively.

obtain good bacterial growth in the filter it is necessary to provide an adequate supply of oxygenated water and a large surface area. A good flow of water through the filter should provide plenty of oxygen, particularly if it is directed onto the media via a spray bar. In large filters, aquarium air stones can be used to aerate the water before, or during, its passage through the biological media.

The biological filter medium should provide a very large surface area in order to ensure that enough bacteria can grow in the filter to decompose

Chemical Filtration

Chemical filter media such as zeolite can be added to the filter to actively remove certain harmful chemicals. If used, they should be placed at the end of the filtration process, after both the mechanical and biological filtration.

Chemical media work by actively absorbing certain chemicals from the water. There are a limited number of sites where this absorbtion can occur therefore eventually the chemical media will become exhausted and will no longer function effectively. This may take from a few days (in a polluted pond) to several months (in a mature pond). Zeolite can be reactivated by placing it in a concentrated salt solution (6 ounces of salt per gallon of water) for 1-2 days and then carefully rinsing in freshwater before replacing it in the filter.

Vegetable Filtration

The biological filter will decompose organic material and produce nitrate. In a natural pond with large quantities of healthy plants these nitrates will be used as a food source.

If there are insufficient plants, the nitrates may be used as a food source by algae resulting in "green water" or dense growths of blanket weed. Alternatively, if the algae are

A vegetable filter using watercress to remove nitrates. Photo: D. Pool

being controlled, the nitrate concentration in the pond may start to adversely effect the fish and plants. Adding fast-growing plants (eg Elodea) into the pond will reduce the nitrate level, however this may not be possible if Koi are kept in the pond as they will uproot and consume the plants. In this situation a vegetable filter may be used. This involves adding fast-growing plants (eg watercress) to the last chamber of the filter, or to a causeway carrying water from the filter back to the pond. The watercress will grow very rapidly maintaining clear water of good quality - and providing salad material for your family (and neighbours!). Plant the watercress by lodging the roots under stones. Don't place it in a planting medium as the roots will absorb nutrients from the medium, instead of forcing the leaves to remove the water borne chemicals.

Ultra Violet Units

Ultra Violet (UV) light is widely used to control suspended algae and therefore keep the pond water clear. These units are very effective, but should be used in conjunction with a filter which will remove the clumped or dead algae. When used, the nitrate concentration in the pond should be monitored since it may rise rapidly when no algae are present to utilise it. Blanket weed growth may also increase due to it utilising the increased nutrient levels. The UV unit is best placed just

An external box filter, in this case combined with a UV unit, is the most popular form of filtration. Photo: D. Pool

after the pump, to ensure that it receives a constant flow of water. The UV bulb needs changing at regular intervals, usually once or twice a year depending on the type used. It is important to do this as when exhausted the UV will not effectively control the algae. Regularly cleaning the quartz tube in the UV unit is also important to ensure it works efficiently. Take care not to look directly at the bulb as it can damage your eyes.

Types of Pond Filters

A range of pond filters are available which will help to maintain good water conditions in your pond.

External Box Filters

External filters are undoubtedly the most popular for all types of pond ranging from a small pool to one in which large numbers of koi are kept. The external filters used by most pond keepers are comprised of a plastic box of a size suitable for the pond, which is filled with a series of foam sheets or similar filter media. Water is pumped into the filter by a submerged or external pump. In the top of the filter it passes through a spray bar to oxygenate the water, through the filter media and back to the pond.

The basic external box filter may be greatly improved by a few additions.

For example:

1. The water may first be passed through a settlement area or "sieve" to remove any particulate matter prior to biological filtration.

2. Zeolite may be placed after the biological media in order to remove any excess ammonia from the water.
3. A drain or tap may be placed in the bottom of each chamber of the filter to simplify cleaning.
4. An ultra violet sterilising unit may be added to the pipework entering or leaving the filter in order to control suspended algae.

Maintenance

Maintenance of an external box filter is relatively easy and is essential if the filter is to remain as efficient as possible. The frequency of cleaning depends on a number of factors such as number and size of fish, pond size, filter size, water temperature etc. The reduced water flow from the filter or build up of debris will indicate when cleaning is necessary.

The mechanical section of the filter will require the most frequent cleaning in order to remove the large particles of debris it has strained from the water. In more advanced filters there is a drain in the filter which can be opened to allow the debris to be discharged. If not present the brushes, foam or other area where the debris is trapped should be drained and the filter media removed and rinsed in old pond water.

The biological filter medium (foam, gravel, plastic, shapes etc) will require less frequent cleaning. Often stirring or flushing through with pond water and draining will suf-

Murky water can be the result of overstocking a pond and inadequate filtration. Photo: D. Pool

p. 36/37: Fish only ponds require good filtration if they are to remain clear and pollutant free. Photo: Sakanaya

fice. Never clean the filter medium with tap water as the chlorine within it will kill the helpful filter bacteria.

Internal Foam/Box Filters
Such filters generally use foam as a filter medium, either placed over the pump inflow or in a canister attached to the pump. They are only suitable for small, lightly stocked ponds. In most cases they are quite bulky and so look unsightly in a small pond or take up much water space. They should be attached to a waterproof cord to allow easy removal for cleaning and maintenance.

Maintenance
Regular maintenance of internal filters is essential if they are not to clog and become ineffective. This can be undertaken by removing the filter medium and rinsing in pond water in order to remove excess debris.

Undergravel Filtration
Undergravel filters use a bed of gravel within the pond as a filter medium. A series of perforated pipes are positioned under the gravel and water is drawn through them and the gravel by means of a pump. The gravel itself acts as both a mechanical and biological filter.

A gravel depth of 15-20cm is ideal. A greater depth does not improve the filter efficiency as there is unsufficient oxygen in the lower layers for the bacteria to function. The size of the filter depends largely on the numbers and size of the fish you intend to keep.

In a planted pond 20-25% of the bottom area may be used as a filter - but don't plant the gravel as the roots will block the gravel making the filter less efficient. A gravel diameter of approximately 1cm is ideal for the filter, as it will have a large surface area and not clog too readily.

Maintenance
Regular cleaning of the gravel is advisable to prevent it from becoming blocked. This can be achieved by stirring the gravel and syphoning away any disturbed debris.

There are a wide range of filters available to the pond keeper. The final choice will depend on the space available, fish being kept and cost.

Your local water garden centre should be able to demonstrate most filters and provide invaluable advice relating to your particular pond. Your dealers advice will prove invaluable and will help to ensure that you select and install a suitable filter in the correct way.

THE IMPORTANCE
OF WATER QUALITY

As with all fishkeeping the quality of the water within a pond is vital for the health and survival of the fish and plants. Poor water quality will result in your fish behaving unnaturally, showing poor colouration and being susceptible to disease, while any plants present will fail to grow and become discoloured. In extreme cases poor water quality can result in the death of both fish and plants. In the majority of cases the problems which occur with pond fish and plants can be traced back either directly or indirectly, to poor water quality.

The following aspects of water quality are the most likely to cause problems in a pond.

| pH | Ammonia |
| Nitrite | Nitrate |

Acidity and Alkalinity

The pH of the water is a measure of the degree of acidity or alkalinity with values ranging from pH 1 (acidic) through pH 7 (neutral) to pH 14 (alkaline). It is important to monitor the pH value within the pond because all forms of life, from the fish and plants to algae and filter bacteria can show adverse reactions if kept outside their preferred range, or if subjected to sudden changes in the pH value.

A good balance between fish and plants is important if good water quality is to be maintained. Photo: Tetra

Cement used in pond construction must be sealed to avoid the water becoming dangerously alkaline. Photo: Tetra

Koi and all other pond fish will happily survive in pH values ranging from 6.5 to 8.5, with values from 7.0 to 8.0 being ideal. Outside this range the fish may have poor colouration, show signs of irritation such as rubbing and jumping, and be more susceptible to disease. Plants, if present, will show poor growth and have discoloured leaves. Sudden changes in the pH can also have severe effects on the fish. Such changes often occur following partial water changes or if ground water is allowed to drain into the pond. To avoid such problems it is advisable to test the pH of the tapwater before conducting a water change and comparing it with the value in the pond. If the pH values differ only change a small amount of water so that the difference is greatly diluted.

Gradual pH changes are not harmful to the fish or plants, and in ponds containing dense plant or algal growth, the pH will change quite considerably in a daily rhythm. At night the plants and algae respire, producing large quan-

CORRECTION OF PH VALUES

pH value too high (above 8.5)

Cause	Correction
Unsealed cement in or around the pond	Seal with commercially available sealant.
Run off from garden	Prevent run off entering pond
Limestone bearing rocks in pond or filter.	Remove or seal with sealant
Alkaline tapwater	Minimise water changes. Dilute tapwater with acidic rainwater

pH value too low (below 6.5)

Cause	Correction
Excess organic debris in pond or filter	Remove debris on a regular basis
Filter malfunction	Ensure filter runs continually remove excess debris if necessary
Excess rainwater entering pond	Divert rainwater away from pond
Acidic tapwater	Add limestone bearing rocks to pond or filter

tities of carbon dioxide which acidifies the water. During the day, the plants and algae photosynthesise (using up carbon dioxide and producing oxygen) allowing the pH to return to normal. As a result the pH of the water at dawn is lower than at dusk, but because it only changes gradually the fish and plants are not affected.

It is advisable to check the pH of your pond water at weekly intervals, to ensure that it remains within the ideal values. Always check the pH of your pond and tapwater before adding water to the pond to ensure they are similar.

In all cases the pH should be changed gradually to avoid stressing the fish and plants.

Harmful substances in the pond

Within the pond, fish waste together with any uneaten food and dead plants is decomposed in a process known as the nitrogen cycle. The nitrogen cycle involves the breakdown of fish waste, uneaten food etc, into ammonia or ammonium, ammonia or ammonium into nitrites and finally nitrites into nitrates. Each of these stages is accomplished by means of bacteria in the presence of oxygen. Ammonia,

41

nitrite and nitrate are toxic to the fish, however, in a well established pond where the bacteria in the filter receive an adequate supply of oxygen rich water, they should never reach toxic levels. This is not the case in a new pond or if it is overstocked with fish

Ammonia

The first stage in the decomposition of fish waste and uneaten food is the formation of toxic ammonia and the relatively non-toxic ammonium. Both are easily converted into the other with the ratio of ammonia to ammonium being largely dependent upon pH.

At a high pH (above 8.5)
- mostly ammonia (Toxic)

At a low pH (below 7.5)
- mostly ammonium (Non Toxic)

At levels as low as 0.25mg ammonia per litre of water, ammonia can be lethal to the fish, therefore, regular tests should be undertaken in order to prevent it reaching toxic levels. This can be done easily using an Ammonia Test Kit. In an established pond the ammonia concentration should be very close to 0mg per litre, if it is not suggests that:

a. The filter or pond has recently been set up and has not matured.

b. The pond is overstocked.

c. The fish are being overfed

d. The filter is not functioning correctly.

e. There is excess organic debris somewhere in the pond. Leaves from surrounding trees are a particular problem.

A high level of ammonia in the water will severely irritate the gills

A build up of leaves or other debris may cause acidic water. Photo:D.Pool

of the fish resulting in them having difficulty in obtaining sufficient oxygen. As a result, fish suffering from ammonia poisoning often show rapid gill movements, gasp at the water surface or rub against underwater objects. The skin will also be irritated and may appear pale due to excess mucus production. Such effects are particularly obvious on dark regions of the skin and on the eyes. Ammonia levels in the pond should be measured at weekly intervals, allowing you to detect and correct unsuitable values before they adversely affect your fish. If high values are noted, the water should be tested at 1-2 day intervals.

Nitrite

Nitrite is the second stage in the breakdown of organic material within the pond and is toxic to both fish and plants.

For this reason it should be monitored at weekly intervals and control measures implemented if raised levels occur.

Nitrite can easily and accurately be measured using a Nitrite Test Kit. As far as possible the nitrite concentration should not exceed 0.2mg Nitrite Nitrogen per litre of water. At a level of 0.5mg Nitrite Nitrogen per litre the fish will be adversely affected. The nitrite binds with the blood of the fish preventing it from carrying oxygen around the body. As a result the fish will gasp at the water surface and show signs of rapid breathing as well as having poor colouration, poor growth and being very susceptible to disease.

Raised nitrite levels are often an indication of excess organic materi-

p. 44/45: Good water quality is essential for healthy fish. Photo: Tetra

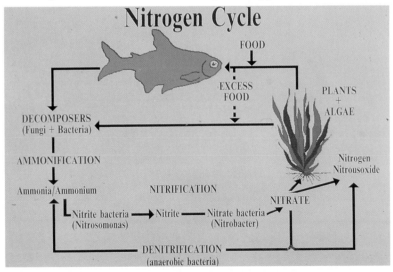

43

al in the pond, or inefficient filter functioning. The cause of such problems are the same as those described for ammonia. Nitrite levels in the pond should be monitored at weekly intervals, allowing you to detect and correct raised levels before they adversely affect your fish. If high values are noted the water should be tested at 1-2 day intervals.

What to do if the ammonia or nitrite content is too high

The accumulation of ammonia or nitrite beyond safe levels reflects a build up of organic impurities in the pond water. To avoid the fish and plants being adversely affected the following steps should be undertaken.

1. Immediately change up to one third of the water in order to remove some of the toxic ammonia. At the same time remove as much debris (eg leaves, uneaten food and dead algae) as possible from the pond. This can be achieved using a pond vacuum, syphon, or a fine net. The replacement water should be the same temperature as that in the pond and be conditioned using TetraPond AquaFin to remove potentially dangerous chlorine.
2. Increase the aeration if possible.
3. Check the pond is not overstocked
4. Ensure the filter is functioning effectively and is not blocked. Clean if necessary using old pond water. Do not use tapwater as the chlorine will kill the helpful bacteria.

5. Avoid overfeeding. Only feed the fish on foods from the nutritionally balanced Tetra Pond range. Feed the fish 2 or 3 times each day when water temperatures are above 8°C but only add the amount they can consume within a few minutes.

Nitrate

Nitrate is the final product of the decomposition of organic material and is actually produced by an effectively functioning biological filter. In the pond nitrates are consumed by plants and algae as a source of food. If the balance between plant and fish numbers is suitable the nitrate concentration will remain at a low level, however, if no plants are present, the pond is overstocked or the fish overfed, the nitrate levels can become raised.

In comparison to nitrite and ammonia, nitrates are considerably less harmful to the fish and plants. However, concentrations of 50mg Nitrate per litre of water which persist for long periods can have adverse effects on the fish and encourage unsightly algal growth. Fish fry are particularly susceptible, and high nitrate levels can retard growth and prevent proper fin development. The colouration of adult fish may also be affected, and the fish will be more susceptible to disease.

By far the greatest problem in a pond resulting from high nitrate levels is the growth of suspended algae

Excess algal growth causing green water is often a result of raised nitrate levels.
Photo: D. Pool

(green water) or blanket weed. These algae increase to troublesome levels if high nitrate levels occur. Raised nitrate levels often occur if an Ultra Violet sterilising unit is used in the pond to maintain clear water. This is due to the UV unit killing the suspended algae which were utilising the nitrates and keeping the concentration at low levels.

What to do
if the nitrate levels are high
If the nitrate levels are greater than 50mg/litre it is advisable to undertake the following steps in order to reduce the concentration.

1. Undertake a partial water change. Test the tap water beforehand to ensure the nitrate concentration is less than that in the pond. Remember to use TetraPond AquaFin to remove potentially dangerous chlorine.
2. Remove excess debris from the pond and filter
3. Encourage healthy plant growth, particularly of fast growing oxygenating plants. In a koi pond where plants are not present a vegetable filter containing watercress can be used. A vegetable filter is simply a container into which water from the filter flows, and in which fast growing plants are added.
4. Ensure that your pond is not overstocked with fish.
5. Do not overfeed the fish. Use the nutritionally balanced Tetra

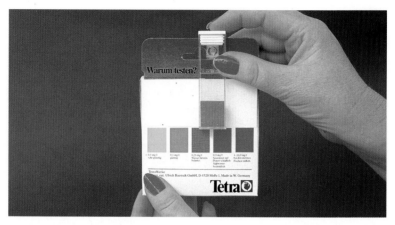

Regular water testing is advisable to ensure that conditions are suitable for your fish.
Photo: Tetra

foods, feeding 2-3 times each day on as much as is consumed within a few minutes. Do not feed when the water temperature falls below 8°C.

Pollutants

There are many forms of pollution which can, on occasion, cause problems in a garden pond and result in the death of fish or plants.

Garden pesticides and weedkillers are a drastic example of this. Both will kill the fish and all other aquatic life very quickly therefore it is important to prevent them from entering the pond. This can be achieved by not using sprays in the immediate vicinity of the pond and not using them at all in windy conditions. It is advisable to ask your neighbours to do likewise. Try to use chemicals which are deactivated on contact with the soil. If it is

absolutely necessary to spray plants close to the pond, only do so on still days and use a large board to shield the pond from any droplets.

Oil and petrol is also directly toxic to aquatic life causing the fish to gasp before they are killed. Even at sub lethal concentrations it will form a film on the water surface preventing oxygen uptake.

Metal poisoning can occur if copper piping, galvanised mesh or metal objects are placed in the pond. Such effects tend to be long term, resulting in poor growth, susceptibility to disease and poor breeding success.

If you suspect a problem with pollutants it is important to conduct a large partial water change to immediately dilute the chemicals. Also remove as much debris as possible as this can compound the problem,

Beautiful and healthy fish is the result of good water quality. Photo: Tetra

and obviously prevent further pollutants entering the pond. Using chemical filter media such as zeolite or active charcoal will absorb much of the pollutants, however it will be necessary to discard the media after use. If the fish are affected remove the worst individuals to a separate container filled with clean, dechlorinated water and add cooking or pond salt at the rate of 1 ounce per gallon of water. The fish can be left in this container until they show improvement.

Tapwater

The most widely used and convenient source of water for the pond is from the tap. However, tapwater is specially treated to make it safe for human consumption and some of the additives, eg chlorine, are potentially very toxic to the fish, plants and filter bacteria.

In natural waters, chlorine is only found in extremely low concentrations, but it is added to domestic tapwater to kill harmful organisms which might affect human health. More toxic chloramines are also used in some areas where the disinfectant needs to stay in the water for a longer period of time. Fluorides which may be added to the tapwater to improve dental health are not toxic to the fish.

49

Compared with the natural environment, the heavy metal concentrations found in our domestic supply may amount to a hundred or even a thousand times increase. These heavy metals, such as copper, zinc and lead gradually accumulate in aquatic organisms and can pose a threat to their health and survival. The high concentrations in tapwater are principally caused by the water coming into contact with lead or copper pipework and are a particular problem in areas which have soft acidic water, or if there is any old pipework in the house.

Fortunately the tapwater can be made safe for all pond life by treating it with a good quality dechlorinator such as TetraPond AquaFin. This should always be used to treat the tap water before it is added to the pond to avoid any adverse effects of the chlorine.

If water quality problems occur it is worth checking initially with an accurate range of water test kits such as those in the TetraPond Test Range.

Testing to identify other pollutants is more difficult and more expensive. In most cases following the treatment outlined above will help. If, however the problem persists your water can be analysed by water authorities or public analysts.

PLANTING THE GARDEN POND

Carefully planting a garden pond with a range of different plants will greatly improve its appearance, particularly if flowering species such as water lilies and iris are included. However the benefits of the plants extend far beyond this. During daylight hours they actually produce oxygen and use up potentially dangerous carbon dioxide in a process known as photosynthesis. The production of oxygen is particularly important to the fish on warm still days. Plants with large or floating leaves provide shade and shelter for the fish, whilst other species may be consumed or provide a spawning medium. Very importantly the plants also use up nutrients and absorb sunlight which would other-

Water lilies form the centrepiece of any pond. Photo: K.A. Frickhinger

wise encourage unsightly growths of algae. Encouraging healthy plant growth will therefore have many benefits for your pond.

Planting

The most convenient and best way to grow pond plants is to place them in a suitably sized plastic container. Planting in a container keeps the plants in tidy bunches; allows the plants to be moved or removed during pond cleaning; reduces nutrient leakage into the water where it encourages algae; and prevents the fish stirring up any mud and clouding the water.

Commercial plastic containers are available in a range of sizes to suit the needs of most pondkeepers. The containers are usually perforated, and should be lined with hessian (provided it is not treated with preservatives), or one of the commercially available liners to prevent the soil being washed away. Given suitable water conditions, aquatic plants will grow in almost any planting medium. Unfertilised garden soil is ideal and should be mixed with fine gravel in the ratio of 3 soil;1 gravel. Commercially available aquatic soils are also ideal for water lilies and all aquatic plants. Using rich soil or manure in the containers will produce healthy plant growth, but the excess nutrients will also encourage algae and therefore should be avoided. Special fertilisers such as TetraPond Lily-Fin are available to encourage healthy growth of lilies and marginal plants and should be placed in the rooting medium close to the base of the plant. These fertilisers are rich in phosphates and contain few nitrates, consequently they will not encourage algal growth. They will greatly increase the numbers of blooms on water lilies.

The upper surface of the planting container should be covered with a one inch (2.5 cm) layer of coarse gravel to prevent the fish digging and uprooting the plants or clouding the water. Larger stones can also be used to hold down the root systems of lilies and some marginal plants.

Containers are available in a range of sizes. As a general rule a small basket (8" x 8", depth 4" - 20 x 20 x 10 cm) can be planted with 1 pygmy water lily, 4-6 oxygenating plants or 1 marginal plant. A medium basket (10" x 10" X 6" - 25 x 25 x 15 cm) will hold 1 small water lily, 2 marginal plants of the same variety or 10-12 oxygenating plants. A large basket (12" x 12" x 8" - 30 x 30 x 20 cm) will hold 1 medium water lily, 3 marginal plants of the same variety or 15-20 oxygenating plants.

Types of Plant

There are four groups of plant which are suitable for the garden pond. The quantities of each plant to add to your pond depends largely on water depth, water surface area and of course personal preferences.

Submerged or oxygenating plants

This group of plants includes the Pond Weeds *(Elodea, Calitriche, and Ceratophyllum)*, Water Hawthorn *(Aponogeton distachyus)* and Water Milfoil *(Myriophyllum)*. Each of these plants will form attractive growth under the water, but their main function in the pond is to consume minerals and nutrients which would otherwise allow algal growth.

Submerged plants are usually purchased as a bunch of unrooted cuttings held together with a lead planting weight or elastic band. Before planting check that the cuttings have not been crushed by the planting weight. If they have remove the damaged portion and carefully replace the weight. The oxyge-

Canadian pond weed (Elodea canadensis) grows rapidly consuming the nutrients which would otherwise be used by troublesome algae. Photo: B. Kahl

nating cuttings are planted in bunches of 5-10 cuttings by placing them in a hole approximately 2 inches (5cm) deep and firming the media with your fingers. Ensure the weight is placed below the surface of the planting media.

Alternatively a bunch can be placed horizontally on the medium and a stone placed in the middle of the cuttings to hold them down. As a rough guide 1 bunch of submerged plants should be added for every 2 square feet (0.25m²) of water surface. Many oxygenating plants are very vigorous growers and it may be necessary to trim them 1-3 times each year to prevent them outgrowing the pond.

Water Lilies

The pride of place in any pond must go to the differing varieties of water lilies. These plants are available in a range of sizes to suit any pond and have been selectively bred to produce flowers throughout the summer. The more spectacular unusual or free flowering varieties are often a little more expensive, but the extra cost is worthwhile particularly when you consider that they are perennial and will produce their flowers for many years. Water lilies are not only attractive, they are also functional additions to the pond, with their large leaves providing protective cover for the fish and shading the water so reducing algal growth. When purchasing water lilies firstly ensure that the variety you select is

A nice clump of water lilies with the leaves lying flat on the water surface.
Photo: Tetra

suitable for the size of your pond. Nymphaea alba, a very common and inexpensive white water lily provides a good example of this. This variety is very vigorous and would quickly outgrow small and medium sized ponds. Unless regularly trimmed it would soon cover all of the pond's surface preventing you from seeing the other pond inhabitants. Most water lilies are well labelled when you purchase them and will have information on the depth of water they should be grown in together with the area of water surface they will cover. As a guide however, a water lily will cover an area of water with a diameter that is twice the water depth in which they should be grown. Colonel Welch (a yellow water lily) for example will grow in water up to 120cm (4 feet) deep and when fully grown, will cover a circle of water surface with a diameter of 240cm (8 feet). The table at the end of this chapter provides examples of water lilies of each colour which are recommended for different sized ponds. It is better to select one or two lilies which are given space to grow well, rather than overcrowd them with the resultant poor flowering specimens.

Having chosen a suitable variety for your pond try to choose potted water lily plants which have a number of healthy leaves, developing flower buds and a pot full of roots. Such plants will grow rapidly and produce flowers in the first year.

Unplanted tubers or unpotted plants are often less expensive, but are unlikely to flower well in their first year. The tubers should be trimmed of excessive roots and planted so that the upper surface or any buds just protrude above the planting medium. They are best grown in 15-20cm of water for several months before moving to their recommended depth. Unpotted plants should be treated in a similar way to the tubers. Dead or damaged leaves should be removed using a sharp knife. Most leaves will, in any case, die back soon after the lily is planted. Placing a large stone on one end of the tuber is often necessary with recently planted lilies to prevent them floating.

If left untended, the water lilies in your pond will increase in size, developing a large root mass and producing many leaves. In time this can choke the pond and result in the leaves being forced out of the water surface instead of lying flat on it. At such times many of the flower buds are hidden by the leaves and the true beauty of the lily is not seen. If your water lily gets into this condition it is necessary to thin it. This operation can be undertaken at anytime, but is best done in March, April, September or October. To thin a water lily remove the planting basket containing your lily from the pond and select one or two strong growth crowns on the same piece of tuber. These should be left in position and undisturbed during the thinning. Trim off the remaining tuber using a sharp knife, leaving at least 8-10cm of tuber either side of the crown. The surplus lily should be removed and the basket filled with planting medium or unfertilised garden soil. The excess tubers can be split into short lengths, each with a growth crown and potted as described above.

When siting your water lilies within the pond make sure they are not subject to excessive water movement or any spray (from waterfalls, fountains or hose pipes). Both will restrict the growth of lily and cause leaf damage. In addition any flowers which are exposed to spray will have a much shorter life - often only a single day.

Floating Plants

Although there are many species of floating plants which can be added to the pond, many will grow out of control and cause problems in the

future (eg Duckweed and Azolla). Two suitable plants are the Water Hyacinth *(Eichhornia crassipes)* and Frog-bit *(Hydrocharis morsus).* As a general rule allow one plant to every 10 square feet (1 m³) of water surface when initially stocking. The plants will multiply but can be netted out if they become overcrowded. The Water Hyacinth is not very hardy and will not overwinter in harsh conditions. To overcome this, individual plants can be overwintered indoors or new plants bought each spring.

Frogbit (Hydrocharis morsus) a small floating plant that will thrive in most ponds. Photo: K.A. Frickhinger

Do not add duckweed to the pond as it will quickly spread and cover the entire surface. Photo: D. Pool

Marginal Plants

Marginal plants grow in the shallow water around the edge of the pond, where their roots are submerged but the stems and leaves are above the water. Suitable species for the pond

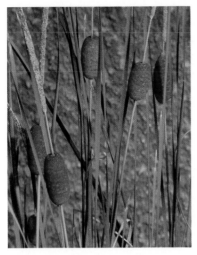

Dwarf reed mace (Typha minima) an unusual marginal plant that is ideal for small to medium sized ponds.
Photo: K.A. Frickhinger

The marsh marigold (Caltha palustris) a hardy marginal species that flowers early in the Spring.
Photo: K.A. Frickhinger

include the Sweet Flag Iris *(Accorus calamus),* Flowering Rush *(Butomus umbellatus)* and Marsh Marigold *(Caltha palustris).* Marginal plants will remove some nutrients from the pond, but their main function is to provide an attractive background against which the pond can be viewed. The stocking rate for marginal plants is determined by the pool perimeter and the surroundings. Try to select plants which will not outgrow your pond. The table provides a guide to the size of the more common marginal plants. Most marginal plants are at their best if planted in groups of each species. Don't plant them too close together as they will spread quickly. If marginal plants are overcrowding their planting container they can easily be divided. This is best done in late autumn or, as a second choice in early spring. Simply tip out the contents of the container, divide the tubers using a sharp knife ensuring there is one bud or shoot on each length of tuber, and replant with the shoots pointing upwards. The use of TetraPond LilyFin in the planting medium will get the young plants off to a good start.

In many ponds the margins of the pond can be extended to form a marsh area in which a number of unusual but hardy plants can be grown. Such an area also forms a nice transition from the water to dry land making the pond look more natural.

Planting the pond surrounds
Don't stop with the pond when deciding on suitable plants, the surrounds are also important. Careful

57

Irises can form an impressive display around the pond. Photo: Tetra

selection of plants around your pond will ensure that it ties in with the rest of the garden. The pond surrounds will also be reflected in the pond surface, adding a further dimension to water gardening.

Almost any plant can be grown around the pond, although it is wise to avoid vigorous shrubs or trees as the roots can damage pond liners and the leaves will be a problem when they are shed in the autumn. Try to select plants so that you have flowers throughout the year. One way to do this is to visit your garden centre every month and see what is in bloom. Then choose those which are most suitable for your pond surrounds - using a reference book if necessary. The choice of plants is obviously very wide but special mention should be made of dwarf trees such as the Japanese Maples (Acer sp.) with their foliage which shows striking colour changes throughout the seasons. Azaleas also have attractive foliage as well as abundant flowers in the late Spring.

Primulas and bulbs provide early season interest, whereas the many species of ferns are a delight throughout the summer and autumn. In the winter don't forget evergreen shrubs, dwarf conifers and plants with coloured stems such as the dogwood (Cornus alba) with its red bark.

MARGINAL PLANTS

Name	Height	Depth of water over roots	Comments/Flowering Season
Acorous calamus (Sweet Flag)	36ins 90cm	0-6 inches (0-15cm)	Green iris like foliage Poker like flowers produced May-July. Very vigorous and self seeding.
Acorus calamus, varigatus (Varigated Sweet Flag)	30ins (75cm)	0-6 inches (0-15cm)	Less vigorous than Sweet Flag. Cream striped leaves. Best planted in clumps. Ideal for small and medium sized ponds.
Butomus umbellatus (Flowering Rush)	36ins (90cm)	1-10 inches (2-25cm)	Tough rush like leaves. Pink flowers produced mid-late summer. Provide plenty of room to encourage flowering.
Calla palustris (Bog arum)	6-12ins (15-30cm)	0-2 inches (0-5cm)	Green "waxy" heart shaped leaves. Small white arum flowers produced in mid-summer, red berries in autumn.
Caltha palustris (Marsh Marigold)	12-24ins (30-60cm)	0-2 inches (0-5cm)	Produces prolific bright yellow flowers in mid to late spring.
Caltha palustris alba (White Marsh Marigold)	10-15ins (25-38cm)	0-2 inches (0-5cm)	Gold centered white flowers produced early to mid spring. Compact plant ideal for small ponds.
Caltha palustris plena (Double Marsh Marigold)	10ins (25cm)	0-2 inches (0-5cm)	Prolific double yellow flowers produced mid to late spring. Compact plant ideal for small ponds.
Carex stricta "Bowles Golden" (Golden Sedge)	18ins (45cm)	0-2 inches (0-5cm)	Golden leaves keep their colour throughout the summer. Taller seed heads produced late summer.
Houttuynia cordata plena (Houttuynia)	6-12ins (15-30cm)	Moist soil to 4ins (0-10cm)	Red tinted stems and green leaves throughout year, white flowers in early mid summer. Move to pond bottom in winter to avoid frost.

Iris laevigata (Japanese Water Iris)	24ins (60cm)	2-4 inches (5-10cm)	Violet flowers in early to mid summer. All varieties ideal for small to medium ponds
variety "Colchesteri"	24ins (60cm)	2-4 inches (5-10cm)	large petalled white flowers which are mottled with purple.
variety "Midnight"	24ins (60cm)	2-4 inches (5-10cm)	velvet blue flowers with yellow streak in each of 6 petals
variety "Rose Queen"	24ins (60cm)	2-4 inches (5-10cm)	Pink flowers - grows best in moist soil.
variety "Snowdrift"	24ins (60cm)	2-4 inches (5-10cm)	6 petalled white flowers with yellow and violet stripe down each petal.
variety "Variegata"	24ins (60cm)	2-4 inches (5-10cm)	Varigated white and green leaves, violet flowers in early to mid summer. Prefers bright sunshine.
Iris pseudacorus (Yellow Flag Iris)	48ins (0-25cm)	Moist soil to 10ins (120cm)	Yellow flowers in early to mid summer. Very vigorous growth therefore not suitable for smal ponds.
variety "Golden Queen"	36ins (90cm)	2-4inches (5-10cm)	Golden flowers freely produced in mid summer. Prefers full sunshine.
Iris pseudacorus varigatus	24-36ins (60-90cm)	0-5 inches (0-13cm)	Yellow/Green striped leaves, yellow flowers in mid summer.
Iris versicolor (American Blue Flag Iris)	24-30ins (60-75cm)	2-4 inches (5-10cm)	Violet flowers in mid summer.
Mentha aquatica (Water Mint)	12-18ins (30-45cm)	Moist soil to 3ins (0-8cm)	Plant smells of mint. Purple flowers in mid to late summer. Invasive, always grow in containers.
Menyanthes trifoliata (Bog bean)	6-10ins (15-25cm)	0-6ins (0-15cm)	Pale pink flowers produced in early to mid summer.

Mimulus guttatus (Monkey musk)	18ins (45cm)	Moist soil to 2ins (0-5cm)	Yellow flowers with red spots from early to late summer. Less hardy varieties include "Lothian Fire" with bright red flowers
Myriophyllum aquaticum (Parrots feather)	4ins (10cm)	3-12ins (8-30cm)	Bright green "feathery" foliage which spreads over pond surface. Move to pond bottom in winter to avoid frost.
Pontederia cordata (Pickerel)	18-24ins (45-60cm)	3-6ins (8-15cm)	Purple flowers produced in late summer. Prefers full sun. Ensure roots do not become frozen
Sagittaria japonica (Japanese arrow)	18ins (45cm)	3-5ins (8-12cm)	Attractive arrow head shaped leaves. White flowers produced in mid to late summer. Prefers bright sunshine.
Scirpus zebrinus (Zebra Rush)	36ins (90cm)	2-5ins (5-12cm)	Banded green and white rush like leaves. Grow in container to restrict spread.
Typha angustifolia (Slender reed mace)	4-5 feet (120-150cm)	2-8ins (5-20cm)	Brown poker heads form in late summer. Grow in large clumps for best effect. Large ponds only.
Typha minima (Dwarf reed mace)	24-30ins (60-75cm)	0-4ins (0-10cm)	Brown poker heads form late summer. Suitable for smaller ponds.
Zantedeschia aethiopeca (arum lily)	18-36ins (45-90cm)	Moist soil 8ins (0-20cm)	Large flowers produced early summer. Move container to pond bottom in winter to avoid frost

DEEP WATER AQUATICS

Name	Depth of water	Comments/Flowering Season
Aponogeton distachyus (Water hawthorn)	6-18ins (15-45cm)	Green oval leaves float on water surface. White flowers with vanilla scent produced throughout spring and summer.
Nymphoides peltata (Water fringe)	6-48ins (15-120cm)	Yellow flowers and leaves float on water surface. Flowers each last 1 day, produced in late summer. Very vigorous growth.

61

| Orontium aquaticum (Golden club) | 6-18ins (15-45cm) | Green foliage held above water surface. Yellow and white poker like flowers produced in early summer. |

OXYGENATING/SUBMERGED PLANTS

Name	Depth of water	Comments/Flowering Season
Callitriche species (Starwort)	6-24ins (15-60cm)	Bright green plant, grows throughout the year. Easily damaged by fish.
Ceratophyllum demersum (Hornwort)	6-48ins (15-120cm)	A hardy plant with brittle dark green leaves. Does not root, therefore anchor with a stone or a planting weight.
Elodea (Anacharis)canadensis (Canadian Pond Weed)	6-48ins (15-120cm)	Very hardy, fast growing plant. May need regular trimming. Ideal oxygenating plant.
Hygrophila difformis (Wisteria)	12-36ins (30-90cm)	Vigorous plant in warmer conditions (over 15°C). Will not tolerate prolonged cold water (below 8°C)
Lagarosiphon major (Crispa)	Up to 60ins (150cm)	Hardy, fast growing plant. May need regular trimming. Ideal oxygenating plant.
Myriophyllum spp (Milfoil)	Up to 60ins (150cm)	Fine feathered foliage. Blanketweed or suspended debris can become entangled in leaves
Potamogeton crispus (Curled pond weed)	Up to 48ins (120cm)	Long crinkled leaves. May take time to establish. Best in ponds with water movement.

SELECTED WATER LILIES - NYMPHAEA

Colour	Name	Depth	Comments
White	alba	Up to 6 feet (2m)	Very vigorous and free flowering. Too big for all but the largest ponds.
	marliacea "Albida"	18-36ins (45-90cm)	Free flowering. Dark green leaves with purple borders. Ideal for medium/small ponds.
	"gonnere"	18-30ins (45-75cm)	A double lily. White flowers with yellow centres.

	x pygmaea "Alba"	6-12ins (15-30cm)	A miniature lily with 1.5in (4cm) diameter flowers. Delicate - avoid frost.
Yellow	Colonel Welch	Up to 4 feet (120cm)	A vigorous lily suited only to large ponds. Only produces few flowers.
	x marliacea "Chromatella"	18-30ins (45-75cm)	Very popular free flowering lily. Ideal for medium sized ponds. Leaves mottled blue or green.
	odorata "Sulphurea"	12-24ins (30-60cm)	Flowers held above water. Given a warm sunny position it will flower freely.
	x pygmaea "Helvola"	6-12ins (15-30cm)	The most popular miniature lilys. Free flowering. Brown mottled green leaves.
Pink	x marliacea "Carnea"	Up to 5 feet (150cm)	A strong growing lily producing blooms throughout the year.
	Mrs Richmond	12-30ins (30-75cm)	Large flowers produced freely. Not suitable for small ponds.
	"Rose Arey"	18-30ins (45-75cm)	A vivid pink lily. Slow to establish - but worth the trouble.
	laydekeri "Lilacea"	12-18ins (30-45cm)	Free flowering variety. Flowers darken as they age. Ideal for small ponds
Red	Escarboucle	Up to 5 feet (150cm)	Free flowering, intense red blooms. Establish in shallower water.
	James Brydon	18-36ins (45-90cm)	A popular red lily producing cup shaped red flowers
	Froebeli	18-24ins (45-60cm)	Free flowering, with apple green leaves. Ideal for small to medium ponds.

SELECTED WATER LILIES - NYMPHAEA CONT/...

Colour	Name	Depth	Comments
Red	x pygmaea	6-12ins	A miniature lily, producing abundant flowers "Rubra" (15-30cm)
Yellow/Red Changeable	"Sioux"	12-24ins (30-60cm)	The flowers are pale peach when first opened, deepening daily to deep orange pink.
	Graziella	12-24ins (30-60cm)	Pale orange flowers which deepen to red-orange as they age.
	"Aurora"	12-18ins (30-45cm)	Flowers start as yellow, changing as they age, orange and finally orange red to pinky

GOLDFISH, ORFE
AND KOI - IDEAL POND FISH

Although there is a very wide range of coldwater fish which may be kept in a garden pond, the majority of pondkeepers choose orfe, koi or some of the many varieties of goldfish. These species are all widely available and are brightly coloured making them easy to see even if the water is slightly cloudy.

Goldfish *(Carassius auratus)*
The goldfish is deservedly the most popular species of fish kept in garden ponds and few, if any, ponds in this country will not have had goldfish in at some time.

Goldfish were first kept as pets by chinese fish breeders over 1600 years ago. Since that time they have been selectively bred throughout the world to produce the 100 or more different varieties that are available today. Unfortunately not all of these varieties are suitable for keeping in a pond.

Many of the more fancy varieties (eg Bubble eyes, Ranchus and Orandas) are a result of many generations of selective breeding and require the constant conditions which can be provided with care in an indoor aquarium. In a pond the

left and above: Fancy goldfish such as these thrive in the indoor aquarium, but can be a little delicate in the outdoor pond in winter.

Photo: Tetra

temperature variations which occur from day to night will affect the buoyancy of the fishes swimbladder, causing them to float to the water surface or sink to the bottom. The colder temperatures which occur in the winter can also prove lethal.

These fancy varieties of goldfish can be placed in the pond during the warm summer months, but need to be removed when the water temperatures fall below 10-14°C. Such transfers need to be undertaken with care to avoid damaging the fish or subjecting them to sudden temperature changes.

More hardy varieties of goldfish, such as common goldfish, comets and shubunkins can safely be kept in the pond throughout the year. Try to prevent the water temperature falling too low in the winter by minimising any water flow in the water. This will leave a deep layer of warmer water at the bottom of the pond, in which the goldfish will thrive.

Size

In a pond goldfish will grow considerably larger then if kept in an indoor aquarium. Common goldfish for example may reach a length of 4.5cm (18 inches) given sufficient space and good water conditions. Shubunkins and comets are slower growing but can still reach a length of 8-10 inches.

If the pond is overcrowded the fish will not grow to their maximum size, therefore it is advisable to follow the recommended stocking levels of 7.5cm (3 inches) of fish length for every 900cm (square foot) of water surface area. These stocking levels should take account of all fish present, as 1 small goldfish in a pond densely stocked with koi will still not grow.

67

Feeding

Goldfish feed on a very wide range of food items in a garden pond, including large quantities of algae, insect larvae and invertebrates. Unless the pond has a very low stocking level, there will not be enough food to maintain the fish in good condition. It is therefore necessary to provide the fish with a balanced diet such as TetraFin Goldfish Flakes, TetraPond Flakes or TetraPond Sticks. As an occasional treat the goldfish can be given a number of other foods such as brown bread, sweetcorn, prawns and worms.

If fed at the same time each day the fish will quickly learn to recognise their owners as a source of food and rise to the surface to be fed. With care they can also be trained to feed from your hand. Unfortunately this appealing behaviour can also be the goldfishes downfall if your pond is visited by a heron with the fish greeting the herons arrival by rising to the surface to be fed. Goldfish are particularly prone to predation by

Right: Selective breeding has resulted in many different colours and forms of goldfish.

Common carp can be added to the pond, but may uproot and eat plants as they grow. Photo: Tetra

herons due to them being slow swimmers, and brightly coloured. The use of a heron scarer or wires around the perimeter of the pond, or a net over the pond is advisable if your pond is visited by herons.

Colouration
The colour pigments which result in the bright colouration of your goldfish cannot be

Goldfish are ideal inhabitants for a garden pond.
Photo: Tetra

manufactured inside the fishes body. Instead they have to consume foods such as shrimps, snails, algae and insect larvae. In the confines of a pond, natural colour enhancers can be given in diets such as TetraFin and TetraPond Koi Sticks. As the goldfish age their colouration can

GOLDFISH FACTS

Family:
Cyprinidae (Carp Family)

Scientific Names:
Carassius auratus

Origin:
Southern China

First kept as Pets:
265 AD by China, but now found in the wild throughout the world

Introduction to Britain:
Around 1700

Distribution:
Originated in China, but now found in the wild throughout the world

Identification:
Distinguished from koi by the lack of barbels around the mouth (koi have 4, goldfish 0). Crucian carp are also very similar but goldfish have a less deep body and a shorter dorsal fin.

Life Span:
Given good conditions a goldfish will live for 10-20 years. In occasional cases they may live for over 40 years.

Colouration:
Goldfish may have a range of colours from black and brown, through gold to pure white. As they age goldfish tend to become paler.

Size:
Goldfish may reach a length of 20-25cm after 4-5 years. Given ideal conditions they may grow to 30cm and weigh 4,5kg.

An excellent specimen of a Koi of the Kohaku variety. Note the clear outline and intense colouration of the red areas. Photo: Tetra

change considerably. Young fish are often dark in colour, and will adopt their bright colours after 6-8 weeks. Once they reach an age of 4-5 years the goldfish will often start to lose their colouration and gradually become paler. It is not uncommon to find old goldfish that are pale lemon or even white in colour.

Golden Orfe should be kept in shoals if they are to behave naturally.
Photo: Tetra

Golden Orfe *(Idus idus)*

The golden orfe is a very active fish which will add considerable interest to any pond. They contrast well with slower moving goldfish and koi, and spend most of their time just under the water surface searching for any dried food or insects which may fall onto the water.

Varieties available

The golden variety of the orfe is the most commonly available and is the best for the pond, due to its bright

Large koi are best kept in a purpose built koi pond. Photo: Tetra

Koi have been selectively bred to produce a number of different varieties.

Photo: Tetra

colouration making it easy to see. Some orfe are also available which are basically of the golden variety, but which have varying amounts of black on them. These black markings can be in the form of small black spots or larger markings.

Blue orfe are also available. This is a more silver version of the orfe with a bluish back colour. These fish will form a shoal with the golden varieties and will stay just under the water surface. However, unless the pond is clear, the darker colour of the orfe will not be seen, with their presence being shown by occasional splashes on the surface at feeding time.

Size

Golden orfe will grow to a size of approximately 30cm (12 inches) in larger ponds, but will reach less than half that size in a small pond. They are naturally a shoaling fish found in large waters, therefore always keep them in groups of 4 or more individuals. Single fish will behave unnaturally and will be more prone to disease.

Being active fish they require a lot of space to swim and grow, therefore they are best kept in a pond with a surface area of 50 square feet or more.

Sensitivity

Orfe are generally a very hardy species and can easily withstand the cold winter temperatures that will occur in the pond. They can suffer if exposed to a temperature of 1-2°C for long periods, therefore minimising water movement in the winter to maintain a warm deep layer of water, is important.

High temperatures can result in more problems for orfe due to low oxygen levels. Oxygen depletion will affect orfe before other pond fish species, therefore on hot still nights when they are most at risk, ensure there is good water movement in the pond (via a waterfall, venturi or fountain).

Golden orfe are very sensitive to the addition of certain disease remedies, and all of the orfe in a pond can easily be lost following careless treatment. If treatment is necessary ensure that you select a remedy which does not harm orfe, such as TetraPond MediFin. Any remedy which does affect orfe will say in the instructions.

Feeding

Golden orfe will feed on the same diet as goldfish. Small individuals should be given a flaked food such as TetraPond Flake, whereas larger

GOLDEN ORFE FACTS

Family:
Cyprinidae (Carp Family)

Scientific Name:
Idus idus

Origin:
Europe

First kept as Pets:
Around 1910

Introduced to Britain:
Around 1930

Distribution:
Widely kept as pets throughout Europe. Golden orfe are found in the wild in certain parts of Britain and Europe.

Identification:
Easily distinguished from other ornamental pond fish by the lack of barbels around the mouth, elongate shape and short dorsal and anal fin. Similar to the dace (Leuciscus leuciscus) which is native to Britain. Can be differentiated by means of its concave anal fin.

Life Span:
Given good conditions can live for 10-20 years

Colouration:
Golden upper surface occasionally with red tints, pale yellow lower surface. May have black markings.

Size:
Golden orfe can reach a length of 60cm (24 inches) in lakes. Usually 30cm (12 inches) or less in garden ponds.

specimens will consume stick or pelleted foods such as TetraPond Floating Foodsticks. Orfe are ideal inhabitants for a planted pond, as they only eat small amounts of plant material. Even when large they will not uproot oxygenating plants or damage lilies.

If looked after correctly, and given suitable conditions both goldfish and orfe will live for 10-20 years in a garden pond. They will also readily breed in the spring and early summer, providing an area of further interest. Further information on goldfish and orfe is available in the following texts: Fancy Goldfish Culture by F Orme, published by Saiga books Water in the Garden by J Allison, published by Salamander

Koi *(Cyprinus carpio)*

Koi are becoming increasingly popular, with their large size and beautiful colouration appealing to many

The colouration of koi will change as they grow - making selecting good individuals interesting. Photo: Sakanaya

Koi are beautiful additions to a pond.. Photo: Tetra

pondkeepers. As with goldfish, selective breeding has resulted in many varieties of koi in a range of patterns and colours. The colouration, pattern and body shape determine the quality of the koi, which is reflected in the price.

High quality koi are perhaps best kept in specialised koi ponds, where the exact conditions necessary to keep the fish in good condition can be provided. Smaller koi can be kept in an average garden pond, but allowance must be made for their rapid rate of growth and large size. Koi may reach a length of 75 cm (30 inches) given ideal conditions, therefore it is important not to add too many to the pond (1 koi per 2 m² is recommended). In addition

they are bottom feeders and will stir up any soil with large gravel and ensure that the plants are well secured. Plastic meshing placed over the planting baskets is one way of preventing the koi from uprooting the plants.

Ponds containing koi should ideally have a depth of at least 75 cm (30 inches) in order to provide a warmer area of water in the winte.r Given this, the koi will safely overwinter in the pond, although many koi keepers prefer to bring their fish into an aquarium or pond in the house or garage where they are spared the rigours of winter.

If your pond is subject to temperatures below 0 °C for any length of time, some form of insulating cover and/or a pond heater is advisable. Koi will readily accept a wide range of foods, but to ensure that they remain in the best possible health, they should be given a good quality diet such as TetraPond Sticks and Tetra Koi Sticks. They will also consume considerable quantities of aquatic plants and blanketweed so helping to keep the pond clean. The colouration and overall health of the koi is affected by the vitamins and minerals contained in the water. By adding Tetra Koi Vital to the pond it is possible to ensure that the correct vitamins and minerals are present in the water, so keeping your fish in good condition.

Breeding pond fish

Goldfish, orfe and koi will all breed in a well kept garden pond. The fish breeding not only indicates that conditions in the pond are ideal and the fish healthy, but also provides a further area of interest for the pondkeeper.

All of the species mentioned above spawn in a similar manner. In many cases the spawning will occur naturally in the pond but for the more adventurous pondkeeper it is possible to select the parents with desirable characteristics in order to produce offspring of a particular colour or with a different finnage. Pond fish tend to spawn in the late spring

Goldfish eggs on blanket weed. Photo: D.Pool

and summer when the water temperatures rise above 18 °C. The first signs of the impending spawning is the males chasing the females and nudging their abdomens and tails. Often several males will chase a particular female, especially if she is full of eggs. At this time the sexes can also be distinguished visually. The males are generally thinner and have a number of small, pale, raised breeding tubercles on the head and front part of the body. The females may be distinguished by the well rounded abdomen. The chasing behaviour will increase in intensity until the male drives the female into an area of dense plant or blanketweed growth. Here she will release large numbers of eggs, which are immediately fertilised by the male. The adhesive eggs, which are approximately 2 mm in diameter, stick to the plants and algae in the spawning area. Goldfish will eat some of their eggs, but in a well planted pond this number is insignificant when compared to the numbers produced. Interested pondkeepers can remove some of the eggs and place them in an aquarium containing pondwater in order to follow subsequent development of the fry. The eggs will hatch after 2-5 days (depending on water temperature) and the fry will cling to any plants or algae. At this stage the fry feed on their yolk sacs and so do not need feeding. 2-3 days later, when they become free swimming the fry will begin to actively search for food. In the pond this is present in the form of microscopic animals. In the aquarium mature pondwater should be added several times a day, or alternatively newly hatched brineshrimp should be given. After 4-5 days the fry will be large enough to accept TetraBaby Fish food for Egglayers. This may be given 3-5 times each day, but take care not to overfeed and pollute the water. In the aquarium regular partial water changes and filtration using a foam filter (eg Tetra Brillant) will help to maintain good water quality. As the fry grow they can be given finely crumbled TetraFin Goldfish food.

In an aquarium ensure that the fry do not become overcrowded as they grow. If you aim to keep the stocking rate at a maximum of 2.5 cm (1 inch) of fish to every 150 cm² (24 square inches) of water surface, the fish should grow rapidly. This may necessitate removing some fish from the aquarium. You should aim to keep the best specimens, so place the surplus back in the pond, or give them to a fellow pondkeeper.

The colouration of the fry may change dramatically as they grow. When small they are usually a brown colour, but they may change to the colour of their parents or grandparents during the first 4 years of life.

UNUSUAL COLDWATER FISH FOR THE GARDEN POND

The majority of ponds are stocked with some of the many varieties of goldfish or, to a lesser extent, with koi. There is no doubt that such displays can look very impressive and be very interesting, but there is no need to restrict yourself to the fish already mentioned. There is, in fact, a very wide range of fish originating from temperate conditions which would be suitable for ornamental purposes. Some such as the red shiner *(Notropis lutrensis)* or blue spotted sunfish *(Enneacanthus chaetodon)* can match the vivid colouration of any tropical fish; others have unusual and interesting behaviours (e.g. 3 spined stickleback - *Gasterosteus aculeatus); while* others such as channel caffish *(Ictalurus punctatus)* and grass carp *(Ctenopharyngodon idella)* grow very big and very friendly. I will introduce some of the many available species here, but a trip to your local aquarist shop would allow you to view other specimens which would add to the variety and interest in your pond or aquarium. The 'coldwater' fish which are available can, for the sake of convenience, be divided into those species originating from Britain and Europe, North America and the Far East.

Golden tench form an interesting addition to the pond. Photo: Tetra

British and European species
Most of the native British fish can be kept in aquaria in their juvenile stages if care is taken with the water conditions. Most of the suitable species for captivity are commonly available from aquarist shops and include carp *(Cyprinus carpio)*, tench *(Tinca tinca)*, rudd *(Scardinius erythrophthalmus)*, minnows *(Phoxinus phoxinus)* and bitterling *(Rhodeus sericeus)*. Bitterling *(Rhodeus sericeus)* are worthy of a special mention because of their very unusual reproductive behaviour. These beautiful little fish protect their eggs by laying them in the gill cavities of freshwater mussels. To do this the female develops a long ovipositor when ready to spawn. This is inserted into the excurrent siphon of the mussel and the eggs are released.

The brilliantly coloured male hovers over the incurrent siphon and

Rudd, (Scardinius erythrophthalmus)

Minnow, (Phoxinus phoxinus)

Tench, (Tinca tinca)

Bitterling, (Rhodeus sericeus amarus)

ing bitterling is very simple as they are tolerant of all but the extremes of pH and water hardness and will readily accept flaked foods such as TetraFin Goldfish food. In a pond they tend to be surface feeders and so will be seen even in the unfortunate event of the water going green with algae. The breeding described above occurs throughout the summer months. During this time the male is very brightly coloured and easily distinguished from the female. The fish will breed readily in captivity providing a mussel is present.

releases his milt. The respiratory action of the mussel carries the sperm into the gill chamber where fertilisation occurs. The fry remain in the mussel until they are free swimming, when they pass out through the excurrent siphon. Keep-

NORTH AMERICAN SPECIES

There are in excess of 100 species of American fish which are suitable for pond and aquarium life. Amongst the most popular and widely available are the red shiner *(Notropis lutrensis)* and the sunfishes *(Lepomis* and *Enneacanthus species).*

83

Some tropical species such as platies can be placed in the pond during the summer months. Photo: Tetra

but tend to be more susceptible to parasitic infection. A wide range of temperatures can be tolerated but those over 22 °C should be avoided if possible as such conditions will shorten the lifespan (normally around 5 years). Feeding is straightforward, with them readily accepting flaked and stick foods. As with the bitterling, red shiners will spawn over a prolonged period of time given suitable conditions (clean water and a temperature of 18-22 °C). Because of the brilliance of the males during spawning, it is worth ensuring that these conditions occur as often as is possible. The male can also be distinguished by the presence of an inverted dark triangle just behind the gills and by the breeding tubercles which occur on the head during the breeding season. Spawning occurs over an area of coarse gravel. The male defends a small territory over the gravel, but following spawning he rapidly loses interest and moves away.

Red shiner *(Notropis lutrensis)*
This species occurs naturally in the south and south west of the USA. Because of its popularity as a bait for larger piscivorous fishes, the red shiner is bred commercially in large numbers and so it is often available within the aquarist trade.

The intense red colouration which occur on the flanks of the male during the breeding season, give rise to it's common name together with more misleading names such as Asian or African fire barbs.

The red shiners prefer neutral to slightly alkaline water with a medium to moderate hardness. They will survive in softer more acidic water,

Sunfishes *(Lepomis spp. and Enneacanthus spp.)*
The most commonly available sunfishes are the pumpkinseed sunfish *(Lepomis gibbosus)*, the black banded sunfish *(Enneacanthus chaetodon)*, the banded sunfish *(E. obesus)* and the blue spotted sunfish *(E. gloriosus)*.

The pumpkinseed sunfish is more aggressive than the other three, and should be kept with members of its own kind or with other large fish.

Given suitable conditions they can reach a length of 24 cm, and at this size they will consume any small fish in the aquarium or pond. Despite these problems, the pumpkinseed sunfish are popular because of their bright colouration (particularly during spawning) and interesting breeding activity.

They breed in a cichlid like fashion, with the male excavating a shallow hollow in sand or fine gravel into which the eggs are laid. The male then guards the eggs and fry until they become free swimming. Because of this territorial behaviour at spawning time, care should be taken not to overstock the pond or aquarium. One male for every one square metre of the pond or per aquarium should prevent any fighting and damage.

The *Enneacanthus* species are often found together in the same habitats in Florida and the Atlantic coast of America. In captivity they are also peaceful, although some aggression occurs between the males at breeding time. As with the pumpkinseed sunfish, they are tolerant of a wide range of water conditions (i.e. pH and hardness) but are badly effected by raised ammonia, nitrite or nitrate levels. Therefore, avoid overfeeding and overstocking and ensure good filtration. Apart from this they are very hardy and are rarely effected by parasites.

The aquarium or pond should contain areas of dense plant growth into which they will retreat when threa-

Pumpkinseed Sunfish, (Lepomis gibbosus)   Photo: A. v. d. Nieuwenhuizen

Sunfishes may be introduced to ponds which are not exposed to very cold winters.

Black banded Sunfish, (Enneacanthus chaetodon)

Banded Sunfish, (Enneacanthus obesus)

fishes to feed. However once they start feeding, they will quickly learn to accept dried foods.

Channel catfish
(Ictalurus punctatus)
Although not suitable for the majority of aquaria and ponds, this species is widely available in its normal, brown colour or as an albino form. Channel catfish are bred in massive numbers in America, where they are an important food fish. In aquarist shops they are usually available as appealing youngsters of 5-10 cm in length. But beware - they can reach a length of 1 metre in the wild and commonly reach 45 cm in ponds and aquaria. At this size they will feed on anything that will fit

tened, and to breed. When first obtained it may be necessary to give live foods in order to tempt the sun-

Brown bullheads (Ictalurus nebulosus) are not good inhabitants of the pond as they will eat any other fish which is small enough to fit into their large mouths.

inside their mouths, including other fish. Consequently they should be kept with members of their own kind or other large fish. The juvenile catfish can also pose problems if kept with fancy varieties of goldfish as they will damage the eyes and fins.

Having painted a rather black picture of the channel caffish, it is only fair to add that they are interesting and intelligent fish which quickly learn to recognise their owner. Water quality is not a problem, as they will tolerate a wide range of pH, hardness and oxygen values. In addition, they are able to resist the majority of parasites which can affect other coldwater fish.

White Cloud mountain Minnow,
(Tanichthys albonubes)

FAR EASTERN SPECIES

Two notable examples of fish originating from the Far East are the goldfish and koi. However, there are

The paradise fish (Macropodus opercularis) thrives in the garden pond during summer months. *Photo: Tetra*

also a number of other species. Included in these is the grass carp *(Ctenopharyngodon idella).* This species feeds to a large extent on aquatic plants and algae, and is often introduced into the pond to control unwanted vegetation. The grass carp is also an interesting fish in its own right. In the wild it can grow to 1.25 m and weight 35 kg, however it is unlikely to reach one twentieth of that in most ponds. Because of their large size and longevity, grass carp can become very tame and will readily feed from their owners' hand. They are also very peaceful, making them ideal companions for koi and large goldfish. In a pond they will help to reduce the algal and plant growth, however to achieve complete control they need to be stocked in reasonable numbers (which would restrict the numbers of other fish which could be kept). In most ponds the diet should be supplemented with a pelletted or stick diet (such as TetraPond Sticks).

As you can see the choice of fish for your pond is not limited to goldfish, koi or orfe. In this chapter we have examined the more unusual species of coldwater fish which are commonly available in aquarist shops. Many other species are suitable and are occasionally available commercially. These include tropical species such as paradise fish, *(Macropodus opercularis),* white cloud mountain minnows *(Janichthys albonubes),* guppies *(Poecilia reticulata)* and some Killifishes.

Hopefully you will now give these species a chance and add more interest to your pond or aquarium.

MAINTAINING HEALTHY FISH

Maintaining healthy fish in the pond is relatively straightforward providing a few basic rules are followed.

Water quality is particularly important and has already been covered. In addition the stocking rate, feeding and introduction of new fish are areas where problems may occur. These subjects will be covered in this section.

Stocking levels in the pond

The quantity of fish that a pond can support is governed largely by the surface area of the water, and whether a filter is installed. As a general rule, you should allow one square foot (900 cm^2) of water surface for every 2-3 inches of fish (excluding tail and fins). This figure allows some margin for the growth that will inevitably occur. For koi

the generally accepted stocking level is 50 inches of fish length for every 1000 gallons of water. Both of these figures are for filtered ponds. If the pond is unfiltered they should be reduced by one third. If overstocked, problems can occur, and very rapidly! In an overstocked pond the filter may not be able to cope with the quantities of fish waste produced, resulting in a deterioration in the water quality. This will greatly weaken the fish making them more susceptible to disease. In addition the fish are in very close contact, so if one individual is diseased, it can spread very quickly to the other inhabitants.

Introducing new fish

When introducing new fish to the pond it is important to avoid subjecting them to a large change in water conditions, as this may stress them and result in them becoming diseased. The fish will usually be supplied in a polythene bag, and this should be floated on the pond surface for 20 to 30 minutes before releasing the fish, to allow the temperature in the bag to slowly change to that in the pond. The bag should then be opened and slowly emptied into the pond.

Many problems can occur soon after introducing a new fish because of the introduction of parasites in the pond. This should obviously be avoided if at all possible. Buying healthy specimens will greatly reduce the risk. Choose fish that are active and appear healthy. Avoid those that are gasping at the water surface, breathing heavily, rubbing against underwater objects, are thin, have obvious parasites or are sulking in the corners, on the bottom or on the surface.

Even though the fish may appear perfectly healthy, it may harbour low numbers of parasites which will rapidly multiply once in your pond and affect the other fish. It is therefore advisable to quarantine all new fish, or if this is not possible to treat the fish with TetraPond MediFin. TetraPond MediFin is a safe and highly effective disease remedy which will eliminate the majority of external fish diseases (and does not harm orfe).

The quarantine tank or pond need not be an elaborate affair, and may double as a treatment container. An aquarium is ideal for small to medium sized fish, but if not available a temporary container can be constructed out of a sheet of polythene. An old paddling pool is a useful quarantine vessel for larger pond fish.

Do not site the vessel in direct sunlight as a rapid temperature increase may kill the fish. A cover over the container is advisable to prevent the fish from jumping out and one or

The fish in your pond should rise eagerly to the surface at each feed. If they do not you may be overfeeding. Photo: Tetra

two plastic plants or plant pots should be added for refuge. A filter can also be added to ensure that the water quality remains good (the alternative is to undertake frequent water changes).

New fish should be quarantined for at least fourteen days before being released into the pond. While in the quarantine container the fish should be observed for any indications of disease and treated accordingly. A preventative treatment using Tetra-Pond MediFin is also a very good idea. After the quarantine period is over the fish should be carefully introduced into the pond as described previously.

Additionally the quarantine vessel and all the equipment should be cleaned and stored dry until next needed.

Feeding the fish

In all but the most sparsely stocked ponds it is necessary to provide artificial food to ensure that the fish are well fed and healthy. Tetra produce a range of foods that will provide the fish with the ideal balanced diet. The fish that are commonly kept in ponds, such as the many varieties of goldfish, koi, orfe and rudd are all omnivorous feeders, meaning that they require a diet which contains both plant and animal matter. For goldfish this is provided in the form of TetraFin Goldfish food and Tetra Goldfish sticks. This food contains all of the nutrients your goldfish will require to remain in the best of health and to grow. For larger pond fish there are Tetra Floating Pond Sticks. These sticks are in bite sized pieces for larger fish, and will

With care your fish can be trained to feed from your hand. Photo: Sukanaya

remain on the surface of the water until eaten. For koi, Tetra have formulated Tetra Floating Koi Sticks, which contain all of the nutrients the koi require to thrive, as well as natural colour enhancers to ensure that the koi display their best coloration. Koi sticks can also be used to pro-mote the coloration of other pond-fish.

The amount of food that is eaten by the fish is largely dependent on temperature, with the same fish eating more on a warm day than on a cool one. When feeding the fish it is important to avoid overfeeding, as any uneaten food will rapidly decompose and pollute the pond. As a general rule the fish should be fed 1-2 times a day with as much food as they can consume within five minutes. It is a good sign if the fish rise eagerly to the water surface for each meal. If they do not, they are probably being overfed.

Pond fish will quickly learn to rise to the surface when you approach in anticipation of a forthcoming meal. If they do not, try starving the fish for 2-3 days and then commence feeding with their favourite food at the same time each day. Once the fish realise that you will not harm them and that you provide food, it is a simple matter to get them to feed out of your hand.

At lower temperatures the appetite of the fish will decrease and below a temperature of 8 °C the fish will not require feeding on a regular basis. It is not that they do not feed at temperatures below this, because they certainly do, particularly following a rise in temperature. However, at low temperatures the fish only require very small amounts of food which are easily digested. If your fish look hungry during the winter, add small quantities of TetraPonding Wheat Germ sticks as they are both easily digested and can be removed if not eaten. Feed the fish during the middle of the day when water temperature will be at it's warmest.

SOME DISEASES OF COLDWATER FISH
DIAGNOSIS, TREATMENT AND PREVENTION

The spring and early summer is a time of the year when pondkeepers begin to experience a spate of fish disease problems. As water temperatures rise and the fish stir themselves from their state of semi-hibernation, they are often in relatively poor condition for a number of reasons.

This results in a lowering of their natural resistance to many infections, and fish pathogens (which may have been present at low levels for weeks or months) seize the opportunity to multiply and the result is all too often an outbreak of disease and fish losses.

Fishkeepers are fortunate in that most of the serious and commonly occurring diseases can be successfully treated using one of the commercially available remedies. However, for these treatments to be successful it is important to diagnose the problem at an early stage and to choose a suitable treatment.

Recognising unhealthy fish

The first stage in diagnosing a diseased fish is to recognise when the fish is unhealthy. Factors which indicate poor health include gasping at the water surface, rubbing, becoming darker or lighter in colour, listless behaviour and appearing emaciated.

If these signs are observed it is important to have a closer look at

Healthy koi. Photo: Tetra

the fish concerned in order to determine the cause. The secret here is not to jump to conclusions. Decide firstly why the fish is behaving as it is and then what would cause it to do so. The possibilities can then be investigated to determine the actual cause.

For example, if a fish is seen to be gasping at the water surface, it is gasping because it cannot get sufficient oxygen (there is more oxygen in the water at the surface). This could be due to poor water quality (e.g. low oxygen concentration, high ammonia or nitrite levels), gill parasites or blood parasites. It is then necessary to decide which of these is responsible.

One clue to the cause of poor health can be found in the time of onset and it's rate of spread. There are 3 main possibilities.

1. Only 1-2 fish are affected, and the problem does not spread to any other fish. Suggests a non-infectious disease or malformation.

2. A small number of fish are affected initially, but this number gradually increases. Suggests an infectious disease.

3. Affects all of the fish in the pond, or all of the fish of the same species or size, and occurs very quickly (say overnight). Suggests a water quality problem.

Other clues to the cause of poor health can be obtained by carefully examining the fish for signs of disease or damage. This can be achieved in the pond, but it is better if the affected fish is placed in a polythene bag where it can be viewed from the side.

Sliminess of the skin
During the early spring (as well as later in the summer) fish may begin 'scratching' against rocks and the pond sides or swimming in a listless fashion with clamped or ragged fins. Closer inspection may reveal that there is also a pronounced grey, slimy, film over the body, which is particularly obvious over the eyes. Reddened areas may also occur on the flanks of the body. These symptoms usually point to a disease called 'sliminess of the skin' This is caused by poor water quality or a range of skin parasites such as *Costia, Chilodonella, Trichodina, Gyrodactylus,* etc. which (when present in large numbers) irritate the skin causing excess mucus production (hence the name of the disease). Sliminess of the skin can cause mortalities or weaken the fish so as to permit the entry of other disease organisms. Consequently prompt treatment is vital, either by adding TetraPond DessaFin (sold in the UK as TetraPond MediFin) to the pond itself, or by separating the worst affected individuals into a treatment tank and adding DessaFin or Tetra Medica Contra Spot. When the symptoms of disease have disappeared, the fish can then be returned to the pond.

The typical appearance of white-spot on an infected fish. Photo: K.A. Frickhinger

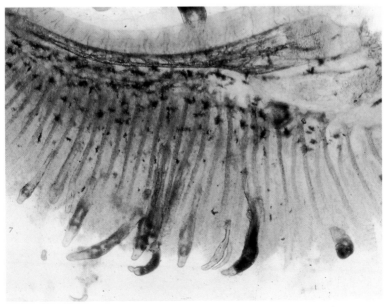

Gill Flukes (Dactylagyrus sp) on the gills of a koi. Photo: D. Pool

Bearing in mind how prevalent this disease is during the spring, some pondkeepers add a preventative dose of DessaFin to the water as soon as temperatures begin to rise. Sometimes coincident with sliminess of the skin, or on its own, the dreaded white-spot or 'Ich' *(Ichthyophthinus)* may strike. White spot is fairly easy to diagnose and must be all too common to many fishkeepers. Small, white cysts about the size of a pinhead occur on the skin, fins and gills in ever increasing numbers.

The speed with which the infection spreads depends on temperature, and is quite rapid at above 12-15 °C. As with many external parasite infestations, a rapid spread from fish to fish is also aided by the high stocking levels in most ponds.

Left untreated 'Ich' can kill fish, either directly or by the secondary invasion of lesions by bacteria and fungus. Because the white spot parasite, while it is attached to the host, is resistant to treatment, chemicals must be added to the pond water. Then as the 'Ich' organisms fall away from the fish to multiply, they will become susceptible to the treatment and be killed before they can re-infect the fish again. TetraPond DessaFin will effectively control 'Ich' in the pond, whilst Tetra Medica Contra Spot can be used in aquaria.

Gill Flukes

Gill flukes of the genus Dactylogyrus are very common and found on many fish in small numbers. In overcrowded conditions or when the

Fungus infecting a wound on the side of a goldfish. Photo: J. Chubb.

fish are stressed the numbers can increase dramatically and lead to the fish becoming irritated (rubbing against underwater objects and jumping), gasping and showing rapid gill movements.

The effects of gill flukes are exaggerated by poor water conditions, therefore treatment should be combined with a partial water change and the removal of any excess debris.

Fungus

Fish fungus is another familiar problem to pond and aquarium keepers alike. White-grey, cotton wool type growths appear on the skin and fins, often as a result of rough handling, fighting or following attack by some other parasite. The spores which give rise to fish fungus are very common in the aquatic environment - just waiting for an opportunity to cause problems for the unsuspecting fishkeeper! Therefore correct care and the elimination of the factors that give rise to the disease are vital in the prevention of fish fungus.

As soon as pond fish begin exhibiting any signs of fungal attack the pond should be treated with Tetra-Pond DessaFin, or the fish should be removed to a separate treatment tank and the required dose of Dessa-Fin or Tetra Medica Fungi Stop added.

The fish should be held here until the symptoms disappear, or further help sought if the condition persists. Do not leave fungus untreated - it can spread very rapidly, killing a fish within a few days.

The wax like growth caused by fish pox. Photo: D. Pool

Fish pox

Fish pox is a problem which frequently occurs on koi, perhaps less
frequently on goldfish and other
species. The symptoms are a white,
pinkish even grey, waxy growth on
the skin and fins. The growth tends
to appear, develop and then disappear, perhaps to recur at a later date.
The growth is produced by a viral
infection in the cells of the fish's
body. Fish pox is usally apparent in
the spring and early suumer, with
young fish being particulary prone
to infection.

However, fish pox does not appear
to be very infectious and does not
seem to pass easily between fish.
Thankfully the 'disease' (if that is
the right word) is not very patho-
genic and rarely, if ever, actually
does any harm. It is unsightly rather

then dangerous and we must learn
to put up with it for the time being,
since there is no reliable treatment.

Leeches

Leeches are a very obvious, but
probably relatively uncommon, parasite infection of pond fish.

Straightaway it is important to point
out that not all leeches are parasitic,
and there are many free-living scav-
engers which may be found in a
pond.

Where parasitic leeches are seen
attached to fish in a pond, treatment
should be swift, before they build
up in numbers. Commercially available treatments may be added to the
pond, although it is probably a good
idea to also remove the heavily
infested fish to a treatment bath containing 15 level tablespoons of

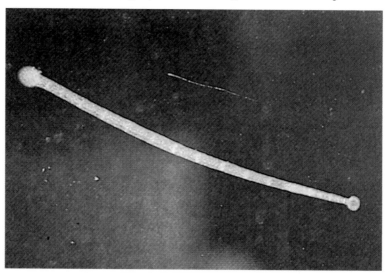

*The fish leech (Pisicola geometra) can be identified by its olive green colour and
paler rings. Photo: J. Chubb*

The fish louse (Argulus foliaceus) will cause severe problems if gets into your pond. Photo: J. Chubb

cooking salt per 10 litres of water (for 15-30 minutes). Those leeches which do not actually fall away from the fish can be removed with forceps. Leeches can then be killed by immersion in boiling water. Because of their powerful suckers, leeches cannot be removed with forceps without first getting them to loosen their grip using a strong salt solution.

Sometimes the above two-pronged treatment fails and if the leeches continue to develop to epizootic proportions, it may be necessary to strip the pond down, clean it out and allow it to dry thoroughly, replace all the plants with fresh and then set it up again. During this time the fish can be maintained in a treatment tank.

Leeches are worth taking seriously.

Not only do they feed on the blood and tissue fluids of the fish, they also transmit certain microbial diseases between fish, and allow secondary invasion with fungus or bacteria at their point of attachment.

Fish lice

Another large fish parasite that no fishkeeper can fail to diagnose properly is *Argulus,* the fish louse. About half a centimetre across, this flattened, disc-shaped crustacean parasite is to be found on the skin and fins of pond fish, especially during the spring and summer. It can move about on the body of the fish, and also live away from the host for short periods.

With its piercing and sucking mouthparts, *Argulus* intensely irritates its fish host, so that heavily infected individuals will often leap out of the water in an attempt to get rid of the lice. Like leeches they also transmit various microbial diseases and the wounds left by the mouthparts of the *Argulus* may become secondarily invaded with bacteria or fungus.

Unfortunately treatment is not straight forward. Commercially available remedies are available which can control the parasite. Fish sensitive to the remedy (e.g. orfe) must be maintained in a separate tank for several days while the pond is treated. During this time, the orfe may be given one or two 30 minute baths in a 10 ppm solution of freshly made potassium permanganate. This should help eliminate any *Argulus* which are present.

A relative of *Argulus,* which may also occur on pond fish from time to time (and especially on newly imported Koi), is the anchor worm, *Lernaea.* Looking like a one to two centimetre long piece of straw protruding from the flanks, fin bases or head region of the fish, this parasite is usually easy to spot, although low level infestations may be overlooked.

Heavy infestations seriously debilitate the host and a reddened, boil-like lesion can develop at the point of attachment.

Treatment is best attempted by:

1. Inspecting each fish and removing the obvious parasites with a sharp tug using a pair of fine forceps. The point of attachment should be anointed with a suitable antiseptic (e.g. 1% Iodine). This process may have to be repeated several times.

2. At the same time as the above, treating the pond with a suitable remedy. Fish such as orfe may have to be kept in a seperate tank (and regularly inspected) for several days while this is going on. Both *Argulus* and

Ulceration on a goldfish, caused by a bacterial infection of a wound.

Photo: D. Pool

Very often an unhealthy fish will suffer from a range of diseases. In this case fin rot, mouth fungus and an internal bacterial infection.. Photo: D. Pool

Lernaea can multiply rapidly in a pond during a warm summer and do untold harm. Hence prompt treatment is vital!

Swimbladder Disorders

Fancy goldfish are particularly affected by swimbladder disorders, which cause the fish to float to the surface or sink to the bottom as soon as they stop swimming. In less severe cases the fish may simply lose its balance, swimming near vertically in the water.

A number of factors can cause swimbladder disorders. Sudden temperature changes can often be the cause, leading to the disorder occurring in early spring or late autumn. If this is when the trouble occurs bringing the fish indoors into an area of constant temperature will help. The problem may also occur soon after feeding. More frequent but smaller feeds will help here.

Ulceration

Various bacteria can cause disease symptoms in fish with the symptoms ranging from sores to a bloated appearance.

Obvious sores or ulceration on the body of the fish may occur following damage to the body of the fish. Infection of the damaged area by Aeromonas bacteria can lead to the wound increasing in size and adversely affecting the fish.

In the early stages ulceration may be treated by adding a suitable remedy to the pond. If the ulcer appears inflamed the fish should be removed from the pond and an antibacterial remedy such as Tetra Medica General Tonic painted on the wound. Keep the concentrated remedy away from the gills and eyes, and do not use on ulcers on or close to the head.

This treatment should be repeated at 2 day intervals until the ulcer begins to heal. The fish should be placed in a container in which 1 ounce of cooking or pond salt is added to every gallon of water. More severe ulceration should be treated with an antibiotic medicated food which can be obtained from a vet.

Treatment

Badly diseased fish should be removed from the pond to a treat-ment vessel, whenever possible, to prevent the disease spreading to the other fish.

If any of the remaining fish show signs of disease it is necessary to treat them in the pond. To ensure the disease remedy is evenly distributed it should be mixed with a small volume of pond water and then spread over the pond surface using a watering can. The removal of any excess debris is advisable as this will bind with the remedy making it less effective.

Treatment on it own is not enough. For long-term effective control you must identify and eliminate the aspects of inadequate pond care which actually brought on the disease in the first place.

ALGAL PROBLEMS
IN THE GARDEN POND

In most ponds problems arise from time to time as a result of algal growth. In many cases the trouble sorts itself out, but in others it is necessary to take remedial action. In the following paragraphs we will look at why these troubles occur and how to overcome them.

Green Water

Green water is a problem that affects most ponds at some time, and if you are unlucky, affects your pond every year for long periods. The green water is caused by minute green plants known as algae which occur in vast quantities when the conditions suit them (bright light and a plentiful supply of nutrients). In some cases, when the pond resembles pea soup, there may be over 10,000 algae in every millilitre of water! That is 50,000 in a teaspoonful! New ponds are particularly at risk, because the nutrients in the tap water provide ideal conditions for the algae.

Benefits

The algae do little harm to the fish, even when the water resembles pea soup. In fact they actually improve the condition of the fish by releasing essential vitamins and iodine into the water. These substances improve the overall health and vital-

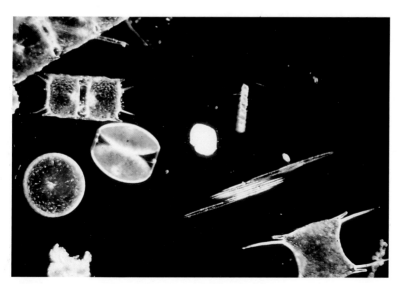

Green water in a pond caused by suspended algae prevents the fish from being seen. *Photo: D. Pool*

Algal cells in the water - each one measures approximately 0.1mm..
Photo: D. Pool

ity of the fish and result in a very intense coloration. Unfortunately in a green pond these benefits cannot be seen. However Tetra have formulated a water conditioner which provides the benefits of green water, without the green coloration. Tetra Koi Vital can be used in any pond, or even in an aquarium to bring out the best coloration in your koi and goldfish, as well as improving their general health and vitality.

Disadvantages

In certain circumstances the green water in the pond can cause problems to the fish. The millions of algae that are present in the water are all respiring, that is taking in oxygen and giving out carbon dioxide. On hot calm nights this can result in an oxygen shortage in the

pond which in severe cases can be fatal for the fish. If you notice your fish gasping under these conditions a partial water change coupled with increasing the water circulation using a fountain, pump or airstone should save them. Such events only occur infrequently and the algae has far more effect on the plants which are starved of both light and nutrients. This results in the plants growing very slowly if at all, and eventually dying. By far the greatest disadvantage with the algae is the fact that they prevent the fish and plants from being seen.

Control

There are several different ways of controlling suspended algae, but one of the most successful is to control the algae using TetraPond AlgoRem

106

and then prevent it returning by encouraging healthy plant growth, adding a vegetable filter (in a koi pond) or providing some form of shade.

TetraPond AlgoRem is a flocculant which sticks the algae cells together causing them to sink to the pond bottom or float to the surface from where they can be removed. By removing phosphates from the water the AlgoRem can also stop the algae from recolonising the pond in the short term.

Once the algae have been controlled the pondkeeper can concentrate on preventing it returning. This is achieved by altering conditions in the pond so that they do not suit the algae ie. by removing the nutrients or the light that the algae requires to grow. Nutrients can be removed by encouraging healthy plant growth and if necessary, adding more plants to the pond. The fast growing oxygenating species are ideal, such as *Elodea canadensis* and *Lagarosiphon major* (Crispa). Add 1 bunch of 6-8 strands of oxygenating plant for every 2 square feet of water surface area. Plant them in planting baskets as this will allow the oxygenating plant to be removed and trimmed to a length of approximately 12 inches (30cm) whenever it starts to outgrow the pond. In koi ponds a vegetable filter such as that described in the section on filtration, should be used. Shading can be achieved by adding water lilies so that their leaves cover 50-70% of the water surface. Tall marginal plants will also help to shade the pond from the morning and afternoon sun.

Many pondkeepers are now using Ultra Violet Light units attached to their filters in order to control suspended algae artificially. Further details on these units is provided in the section on filtration.

Blanket Weed

Blanket weed is not in fact a weed, but is the collective name for several species of filamentous algae. As with the algae responsible for green water, the filamentous algae thrive in bright conditions where there are abundant nutrients. Where favourable conditions exist the blanket weed can grow at a phenomenal rate, doubling its own weight in only 24 hours.

Advantages

To many peoples surprise there are a number of advantages of having blanket weed in the pond. Firstly, it will only occur in water where the ammonia, nitrite and nitrate concentrations are reasonably low, therefore its presence indicates that the conditions in the pond are suitable for fish.

Blanket weed also absorbs ammonia and nitrate from the water as a source of nutrition. Both of these substances are toxic to the fish and plants at raised levels and so the algae actually improves the water conditions within the pond. If prop-

The bad side of blanket weed' choking lily leaves. Photo: D. Pool

erly managed it will act as an ideal vegetable filter, removing the ammonia and nitrate that are produced as the fish waste decomposes. By removing the blanket weed on a weekly basis you can greatly reduce the pollutant levels in your pond.

Most of the fish kept in ornamental ponds are omnivorous, eating both plant and animal matter. This can include large quantities of filamentous algae. Not only this, the algae also provides a rich food source for many invertebrates. Examine a handful of blanket weed from your pond and you are likely to find a range of bloodworms, shrimps, waterskaters and fly larvae all of which are eagerly consumed by the fish, and which keep them going while you are away on holiday.

Blanket weed is regularly used by fish as a spawning medium. Both koi and goldfish will spawn on long strands, often favouring it to artificial spawning media and plants. The algae also provides a safe sanctuary for the newly-hatched fry from their ever hungry parents.

Disadvantaqes

By far the greatest disadvantage with blanket weed is due to it choking everything in the pond. The algae filaments become entangled as they grow and if left unchecked, will block the filter, smother the plants and reduce the area in which the fish can swim. When present in such large quantities the blanket weed can greatly reduce the oxygen levels in the pond, particularly on still warm nights, when the algae photosynthesise rapidly and little oxygen is absorbed into the water. A further problem can arise in the autumn when the blanket weed starts to die. At such times the large

In close up blanket weed is comprised of a mass of tangled filaments.

Photo: D. Pool

quantities of dead plant material will start to decompose and rapidly pollute the water.

Control

Before choosing a method for controlling blanket weed, the pond-keeper should consider the advantages and disadvantages in the pond in question and then decide if eradication is necessary, or whether

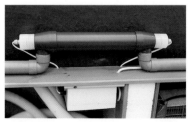

An Ultra Violet unit attached to the filter will help to control suspended algae but may encourage blank.. Photo: D. Pool

reducing the growth would be a better alternative. Blanket weed can be effectively controlled in a three stage process. First, physically remove as much blanketweed as possible by hand, or by winding it around a rough stick. Secondly, treat the pond with a good quality algicide to kill the remaining blanket weed and prevent it returning in the short term. It is important to remove as much blanketweed as possible before treating with an algicide as any dead algae will decompose and can pollute the water. Finally, encourage healthy plant growth to remove excess nutrients and light, so preventing the blanket weed from re-establishing. The plant species and stocking densities to use are the same as those for controlling green water.

A SEASONAL GUIDE TO POND CARE

Once set up there is relatively little maintenance required in order to maintain your pond in good condition and the fish and plants within it in the best of health. The maintenance tasks that need to be undertaken are largely dependent on the season of the year and the water temperature. This will obviously vary depending on the area of the country in which you live, however the activities of the fish and plants give a useful guide to when feeding should begin, filters be turned down, heaters turned on etc. As a rough guide a seasonal schedule of pond maintenance is provided here. A summary of tasks to be undertaken is included at the end of the chapter.

WINTER

Throughout the winter your pond and its fish will be in a state of dormancy and there will be relatively few tasks to be undertaken.

Water Temperature

Pond fish can survive at a wide range of water temperatures including those which are likely to occur in your pond. However, sudden changes in temperature or prolonged cold could have some adverse effects.

Sudden temperature changes can occur on clear frosty days throughout the autumn, winter and spring. On such days the daytime temperature may be as much as 10°C warmer than at night, with the rapid fluctuations stressing the fish and in severe cases causing their death. Such problems are reduced in larger ponds or where there is a water depth of over 45cm since the larger volume of water takes longer to warm up and cool down.

A water temperature of 0-2°C can cause problems for the fish, particularly if it remains at that level for a prolonged period of time. Fortunately this is unlikely to occur in most ponds, even in the most severe winters due to the denser warm water (at 4°C) sinking to the bottom and being insulated by the cooler surface water or ice. Under such conditions the fish will congregate in the deepest (= warmest) part of the pond. A reasonable water depth (45cm or greater) and little or no circulation is important to maintain this warm water area.

Water Circulation

Minimal water circulation throughout the winter is important to prevent cold surface water being mixed with the warmer bottom water and to prevent the fish having to swim to maintain their position. Therefore fountains and waterfalls should be switched off as soon as you stop regularly feeding the fish (when the

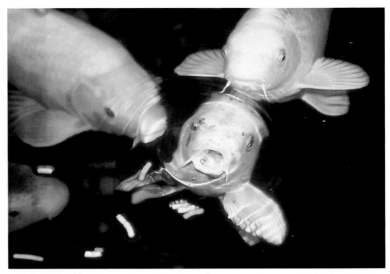

When water temperatures fall below 8 °C only feed the fish on wheatgerm sticks when they are active. Photo: K.-H.Wieser

p 112/113: Throughout the winter the pond should be left to allow the fish to conserve valuable energy reserves. Photo: Sammer

water temperature falls below 8°C). This is also a good time to remove the pump for cleaning or servicing. There is some confusion amongst pondkeepers on the subject of whether a pond should be filtered during the winter.

The advantage of leaving the filter running is that it will decompose some organic matter, even though this will occur at a very slow rate due to the water temperatures. The great disadvantage is the resultant water circulation.

In general the filter in a planted pond can safely be turned off when the fish stop feeding (ie at a water temperature of 8°C). Below this temperature very little waste is pro-

duced by the fish with much of this being decomposed by bacteria in the pond. The filter should be switched on when water temperatures rise to 8°C and the fish are fed on a regular basis. Whilst switched off the filter may be cleaned and the pump serviced.

In a fish only pond (eg koi pond) the pump may be kept running on the minimum flow setting. To reduce water circulation the filter should take water from close to the surface and return it at the surface, preferably directed against the pond side to further reduce turbulence. Many koi keepers also add a bucket or dustbin, placed on its side in the deepest areas of the pond. This

Remove fancy goldfish from the pond before the winter. Photo: Tetra

creates a sanctuary of still, warm water where the koi and other pond fish will congregate.

Ice Formation

The water surface is the place where oxygen is absorbed into the pond and carbon dioxide released to the air. If the surface is covered by ice for more than 1-2 days an oxygen shortage or a build up of carbon dioxide can occur which will adversely affect the fish. Such effects can be prevented by the use of a pond heater which will keep a small area of the water ice free. Alternatively part or all of the pond may be covered. A suitable cover may be constructed using a wooden frame covered in polythene or "bubble wrap" and should be positioned 10 to 15cm above the water surface in order to trap an insulating layer of air. If ice does form it should never be smashed as the shock waves will stress the fish. Instead pour hot water onto the ice to clear a small area.

Feeding

Throughout the winter the water temperature in the pond will fall below 8°C and so the fish will not require regular feeding. During mild spells the fish will rise to the pond surface searching for food. At these times the fish should be fed very small quantities of easily digested foods such as TetraPond Wheat Germ Sticks. It is advisable to feed the fish in the middle of the day when they are most active - but take great care not to overfeed and remove any uneaten food to prevent it decomposing and polluting the water.

Rainfall

Throughout the winter heavy rainfall is likely to occur. Although the small amounts which fall directly into the pond are unlikely to create problems, run off from the surrounding garden should be avoided. Large quantities of rain water can cause a sudden reduction in the pH of the pond, which could stress the fish. In addition the garden run off may be rich in nutrients (eg fertilisers), which can create algal problems in the forthcoming spring. Some thought when creating the pond or a few small alterations afterwards can overcome such problems.

HERONS PREDATION

Every year many pondkeepers lose fish from their ponds following the visit of a heron. The occasional visit of these magnificent birds can create a great deal of interest, but unfortunately they are efficient predators and can decimate the fish population in your pond.

The threat from heron predation can occur anywhere even in the centre of large cities. It can also occur at any time of the year, although the problem is at its greatest in the winter and spring.

Each day an adult heron needs about 13 ounces of food, which is equivalent to 3 six inch long koi, or ten 2 inch long goldfish. Herons are generally shy birds and will visit garden ponds when everything is quiet, which is usually early in the morning or in the evening. Once the herons have found an easy source of food, ie. colourful fish in a shallow pond, they will return on several consecutive days until most of the fish have been taken.

Reducing Heron attacks

There are several ways of reducing heron attacks on your pond fish which can be used with varying success.

Netting the Pond

Suspending a net 15-30cm above the pond surface will prevent the heron attacking the fish. Make sure the net is taut and cannot fall into the pond as the heron may try to land on the net and spear the fish through it.

Suspended Wire

Herons will not normally land directly in the pond as they will scare the fish. Instead they land in the garden and stalk towards the water. Suspending strong fishing line 30-45 cm above the ground all around the pond perimeter will stop the heron getting to its destination. Make sure the fishing line is positioned 15-30cm back from the pond to prevent the heron leaning over the barrier to catch the fish.

A pond in your conservatory is not affected by the weather outside. Photo: D. Pool

p 118/119: In spring Azeleas and Rhodendrons planted around the pond will flower.
Photo: Tetra

Commercial Heron Scarers

Commercial scarers work on the same basis as the suspended wire. When the heron bangs into the nylon thread a loud noise and visual deterrent is triggered which scares the heron away.

Plastic Herons

Artificial plastic herons are very popular and work on the principle that herons are territorial and will not feed close to another heron. Unfortunately this is not completely effective at anytime - and in late winter and early spring when the herons are searching for a mate it actually attracts herons.

Using one or more of the above measures you should be able to prevent herons attacking your fish. If you do lose some fish don't resort to trying to kill the heron. They are a protected bird and anyone killing or attempting to kill a heron could be liable to a substantial fine. In any case it is likely that other herons will replace those that are killed.

SPRING

Feeding

During the spring the days will begin to lengthen and the water temperature in your pond will start to rise. At temperatures above 8°C your fish will become noticeably more active and will begin searching for food. Initially they should be fed once a day on floating foodsticks or flakes.

In later spring the fish will be feeding ravenously in order to build up their strength after the rigours of the winter.

During this time feed them twice a day, taking care that all of the food given is consumed within 5 minutes. Foods containing colour enhancers can also be given from late spring onwards to promote the colouration of the fish.

Disease

As the fish awaken from their "semi-hibernation" they will be very weak and susceptible to infection by parasites.

Watch out for signs of fungus, gasping, scratching against underwater objects or a grey slimy coating to the skin.

Treating the pond with a general external parasite remedy is advisable, although the worst affected individuals should be removed to a treatment container. Many pondkeepers add a preventative treatment to their ponds in April in order to kill any parasites before they adversely affect the fish.

Water Circulation

The pump and filter should be restarted 1-2 weeks before you start feeding the fish. As the water temperature increases the pump output can be turned up and the pump positioned on the pump bottom. Pumps that have been running throughout the winter should be turned up and lowered to the pond bottom.

Regular feeds of TetraPond Sticks will ensure that your fish remain in the best possible condition. Photo: Tetra

p.122/123: In the early spring your pond is likely to be visited by frogs and toads.
Photo: Tetra

Algae problems

Algae growth, either in the form of green water or blanket weed, can be a problem in the spring before the plants become established. Control can be achieved using algae treatments or a UV unit together with increasing the amount of oxygenating plants. Further details are provided in the appropriate chapter. In a well planted pond green water condi- tions will only last for a short time until the plants start to grow and no preventative measures are neces- sary.

New Plants

The spring is an ideal time for add- ing new plants to your pond. The safest and most convenient way to plant your pond is by using the plas- tic baskets available from most

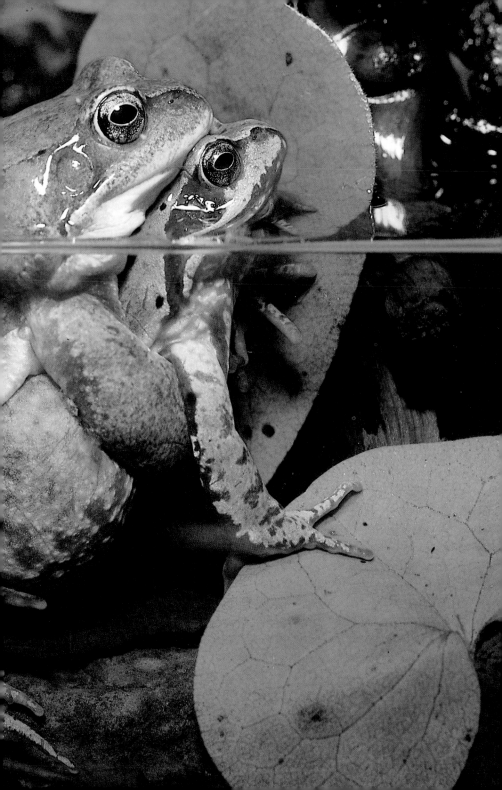

water garden centres. These come in a range of handy sizes and permit the easy re-arrangement of the plants at a later date. The baskets are best lined with clean sacking or netting and then filled with good quality soil or special planting media. Large gravel should be added to the top of the baskets to prevent the fish disturbing the soil and clouding the water. After introducing the plants it is advisable to add a good quality pond fertiliser to ensure they get off to a good start.

Introducing Fish

Now is also a good time to introduce new fish into your pond. Always select healthy, active individuals which show no sign of disease. Avoid those with folded fins or obvious parasites and individuals which are gasping at the water surface or sulking on the bottom. You should also not purchase fish from containers in which other unhealthy or dead fish are present, as they may all be diseased. When you get the fish home it is advisable to quarantine them for 7 to 10 days before introducing them into your pond in order to reduce the risk of spreading disease. A preventative treatment of TetraPond MediFin will remove any parasites present on the new fish.

Blossom

If you have fruit trees in the vicinity of the pond the blossom may be a problem in late spring and it is advisable to place a fine meshed net over the pond. Although the net may look unsightly it only needs to be in position while the blossom is a potential problem.

SUMMER

Throughout the summer the warm weather and increased activity of both pond fish and plants can lead to a number of problems in ornamental ponds. Fortunately these problems are relatively easy to control or better still prevent.

Oxygen

At summer temperatures the major water quality problem is due to a lack of dissolved oxygen which results in the fish gasping at the water surface, showing rapid gill movements and, in severe cases, dying. Such problems are usually confined to ponds in which there is little or no water movement, and generally occur at night. At high temperatures water is not able to hold as much oxygen. Therefore, if there is no water movement to allow the oxygen to be absorbed across the surface, it can quickly be used-up. Such problems do not usually occur during the day because the plants and algae present in the water will be photosynthesising. That is, taking in carbon dioxide and water, and forming carbohydrates and oxygen. This oxygen release will ensure that there is sufficient in all but the most overcrowded pond, throughout the day time.

Throughout the summer you should be able to enjoy the beauties of your pond.
Photo: Tetra

However, after dark the plants and algae stop producing oxygen and instead use it to respire. This, in addition to the continuing oxygen consumption of the fish, bacteria and other pond inhabitants can quickly cause oxygen depletion. Oxygen depletion in an ornamental pond can easily be prevented by ensuring that there is plenty of water movement which will mix the high oxygen surface water and the low

oxygen bottom layers. This water movement may be achieved using a waterfall, fountain or even an aquarium air pump and stone. Excess debris should be removed because it will use up large amounts of oxygen as it decomposes.

Pollutants

The majority of readers will be familiar with the nitrogen cycle, which is the process by which organic waste is decomposed into ammonia, nitrite and finally nitrate. In water some of the toxic ammonia forms non-toxic ammonium. The relative amounts of each depend on a number of factors of which the most important are pH and temperature.

Below a pH of 8.0 the majority of ammonia is present in the non-toxic ammonium form. Above 8.0 the toxic form becomes increasingly more prevalent. With regard to temperature, there is approximately five times as much toxic ammonia at a temperature of 20°C than at 5°C. Whilst this is unlikely to cause a problem in a pond with a pH of 7.5 or less, it could do so in a poorly filtered or overcrowded pond with a pH of 8.0 or above. Symptoms of ammonia poisoning are similar to those of low oxygen, although the fish may also rub against underwater objects. The effects are more severe than oxygen depletion and may result in prolonged poor health in your fish. Raised levels of nitrite in the water are a problem whenever they occur, but can be a particular menace during the warmer weather. Nitrite effects the fish by binding with the blood and preventing it carrying as much oxygen as normal. If the water has low levels of oxygen due to the raised temperature and other factors already discussed, the effects of the nitrite may be greatly exaggerated.

Careful monitoring with a test kit will enable rapid detection of raised ammonia or nitrite levels. Levels significantly above 0mg per litre of water would indicate a poorly functioning filter, overcrowding, overfeeding or a recent introduction of fish.

Such problems can be overcome immediately by undertaking a large (25-50%) water change to dilute the polluted water. At the same time remove any excess debris that has accumulated on the pond bottom. The use of an active filter media such as zeolite which will absorb the ammonia will also help.

Holidays

Many home pond owners are concerned about leaving their pond whilst they are away on holiday. In fact, those worries are unfounded

p. 126/127/128: Both damselflies (126/127) and dragonfliles (128) will visit your pond during the summer. They can be distinguished by the bulbous eyes of the dameslfly and because if folds its wings when it lands. Photo: Tetra

and the pond will come to no harm whilst they are enjoying themselves. In a planted pond the fish will find plenty of algae and insect larvae on which they can feed in order to survive.

Even in a koi pool, the koi will find sufficient algae and other aquatic life to survive without any adverse effects. It is advisable however not to introduce any new fish in the weeks immediately before the holiday as any diseases introduced could cause severe problems if not controlled. Overfeeding just before departure is also not advisable as any uneaten food could pollute the water.

As a precaution, it is wise to ask a neighbour or friend to have a look at the pond occasionally to check there are no severe problems (eg dead fish, pump not working). This person can be asked to feed the fish, but unless they are a fishkeeper the amount to give at each feed should be measured into a polythene bag or envelope. Most non-fishkeepers add too much food to the pond resulting in polluted water and the loss of your fish.

Evaporation

The loss of pond water due to evaporation can be considerable, particularly if you have a waterfall or fountain.

In fact, in extreme cases the water loss can be so great that it can be confused with a leaking pond. If the pond level only drops during periods of hot weather it is safe to assume that evaporation is the cause. A continual drop in the pond level, despite the weather conditions, can be attributed to a leak, which will need finding and sealing. Evaporation losses can be topped up with tap water that has been dechlorinated with a good quality conditioner.

Fountains

Many garden ponds have ornamental fountains which are switched on on hot days or when you are in the garden. In windy weather however they can result in debris from the surroundings washing back into the pond together with water loss from the pond. It is therefore advisable to switch off the fountain whenever the wind is particularly strong.

Fountains have an adverse effect on water lily growth. Water lilies do not grow well if water is falling onto their leaves.

If the water on the leaves evaporates in strong daylight, it can burn the leaves causing brown areas which rot, leaving holes and "tatty leaves". It is therefore advisable to place water lilies away from your fountain and waterfall, to minimise the amount of water falling onto the leaves.

Spawning

In the late spring and summer it is likely that the fish in most healthy ponds will spawn. This does not create any problems at all in the majority of ponds. It is, however, worth looking at the parent fish when spawning is completed to check that they have not been damaged.

Grazes and torn fins will usually heal within a few days, but if there is any sign of infection by bacteria (which cause the wound to become inflamed) or fungus (resulting in cotton wool like growths) treatment with a general external parasite remedy is recommended.

While the fish are spawning the females can be pushed into shallow water or even out of the pond. Obviously it is worth keeping watch over the pond during these times to ensure that the fish do not become stuck.

After a successful spawning, problems can develop due to your pond becoming overcrowded. Such problems generally occur in late summer as the fry grow, and can be identified by the fish gasping and the water becoming cloudy. If such problems do occur it will be necessary to reduce the fish numbers, getting rid of the excess to friends or neighbours who have a pond, or, if you can make the necessary arrangements, to a local aquatic shop.

Perhaps the most common "summer pond problem" is that of excessive algal growth. This subject is covered in a previous chapter.

AUTUMN

Autumn is the time to prepare your pond and fish for the rigours of winter.

Feeding

In September and early October your fish should still be feeding will and you should feed them well to ensure that they build up sufficient food reserves to last them through the winter. Feeding your fish once or twice daily on a good quality flake or stick food will ensure that your fish are in the best possible condition. Continue feeding your fish regularly for as long as they are active.

Once the water temperature falls below 8°C the fish will not require regular feeding. When the fish rise to the surface feed them on an easily digested wheat germ based food, taking great care not to overfeed. Small fry should be given a flaked food for as long as they are near the surface.

Cleaning

The autumn is an ideal time to give your pond its annual overhaul and remove any debris which has accumulated during the year. The cleaning is best done before the water temperature falls below 10°C as the fish will still be active and are unlikely to suffer any ill effects from the disturbance.

p 132/133:During autumn the pond plants will gradually brown and start to die back. Photo: Tetra

The pond should be partly drained (removing say 50% of the water) using a syphon, pump, or pond vac to remove water and debris from the pond bottom. If a normal pond pump is used, large particles of debris should be removed beforehand using a find meshed net, and the pump cleaned afterwards to prevent it from becoming blocked. If the pond is particularly dirty it may be necessary to remove the fish to a temporary holding container and completely drain and clean the pond. Make sure that the water in the container is oxygenated and that the fish cannot jump out. When replacing the water, treat it with a good quality conditioner such as TetraPond AquaFin to remove any potentially dangerous chlorine, making it safe for the fish and plants.

Plant Pruning

When the water is at a low level you have an ideal opportunity to trim back deep water aquatic plants which would otherwise die back during the autumn and winter causing deoxygenation and other water quality problems. The spent blooms and browning leaves of lilies should also be removed. As the first frosts attack marginal plants they too should be cut back and less hardy plants such as water hyacinth moved indoors for the winter. Sensitive marginal plants such as the Arum lily should be moved to the bottom of the pond where they will be protected from frosts by the extra water.

Falling Leaves

In the autumn it is advisable to place a fine meshed net over the pond in order to prevent falling leaves dropping into the water. Although the net may look unsightly, it only needs to be in position while the leaves are falling - and is far easier than removing the leaves from the pond by hand.

Fancy Goldfish

The low water temperatures during the winter can cause problems for the more fancy varieties of goldfish (eg bubble eyes and lionheads), leading to swimbladder disorders and even death. To prevent this it is advisable to catch any fancy goldfish in the autumn and place them in an indoor aquarium. The easiest time to do this is when the water levels are reduced for maintenance.

p 134: A net should be positioned over the pond in the autumn to prevent leaves falling into the water. The net need not look too obtrusive. Photo: D. Pool

POND MAINTENANCE

Month	Pond Maintenance
January/February	Prevent ice covering the entire pond surface by installing a floating pond heater and/or placing an insulating cover above all or part of the pond surface. Do not allow snow to remain on the ice or insulating cover for long periods. Protect your fish from heron attack if necessary. Commercial scarers, a net covering the pond or strong fishing line suspended 45cm above the ground around the margins will help. A clean plastic bucket positioned on its side in the deepest part of the pond will provide an ideal refuge for the fish.
March/April	The heater and/or cover can be removed when the danger of frost has passed. Remove any excess debris that has accumulated during the winter. Algae problems may occur and should be controlled using plants, algicides or a UV unit. If diseases become obvious on the fish treat the pond with TetraPond MediFin. Divide and re-pot plants if necessary. Frogs and toads may visit your pond to breed. Remove excess spawn to other suitable Ponds
May/June	Algal growth may be a problem and should be controlled as described in a previous chapter. Place a fine net over the pond to prevent tree blossom landing on the water. The plants will be growing actively. Encourage growth using water and substrate fertilisers. Buy new plants - choose those which look healthy and have new growth. Do not let submerged plants dry out.

Filter Maintenance

Feeding

In a planted pond the filter can be switched off and the pump and filter cleaned or serviced. In fish only ponds keep the pump running. Position the pump and the filter outflow close to the water surface to minimise water circulation. Turn the pump down to its minimum flow rate. During cold periods place insulation around external filters to stop them freezing. Remove any excess debris from the filter if/when necessary.

Do not feed regularly at water temperatures below 8°C - which should include most of this period. If the fish rise to the surface feed on easily digested wheat germ sticks.

Re-install and start the filter if it was removed during the winter. Weekly testing of the ammonia and nitrite levels are recommended as the filter matures. Regular water changes or the use of chemical media such as zeolite will overcome raised levels if they occur. Pumps which have been running through the winter should be lowered to the bottom and the flow rate increased. Remove insulation if used. Remove excess debris as required.

Once the temperature is above 8°C the fish will actively search for food. Feed them on flake or Floating Foodsticks. Avoid overfeeding. Tempt the appetites of sluggish fish with earthworms or live bloodworms.

Regular cleaning may be necessary, particularly of the pre-filter and mechanical filter section. Do not use tap water to clean the filter media. Monitor ammonia, nitrite and nitrate levels in the pond.

The fish will be actively feeding and should be fed 2-4 times each day on as much as they will consume within 2-5 minutes. Use colour enhancing foods to improve colouration, in addition to flake and floating foodsticks. Treat foods may be given occasionally.

Month	Pond Maintenance
July/August	Prune fast growing plants if necessary. Watch out for signs of low oxygen (fish gasping), particularly in the early morning. If seen increase water movement using a fountain or waterfall and remove excess debris. In severe cases change 5-10% of the water. Replace water lost through evaporation.
September/ October	Remove dead leaves and blooms from aquatic plants before they decompose. Prune submerged aquatic plants. Position a net over the pond to prevent leaves falling in the water. An ideal time to give your pond its annual clean. Remove up to 50% of the water together with any debris. Always use TetraPond AquaFin to condition tap water before it is replaced.
November/ December	Install a pond heater and/or insulating cover if temperatures approach freezing. Measures may also be necessary to prevent heron attack. Add a clean plastic bucket to the deepest part of the pond for shelter.

Filter Maintenance

Feeding

Regular (perhaps daily) maintenance may be needed. Remove excess debris from the pre-filter and mechanical filter.

Feed the fish 2-4 times each day on the same foods as in May/June. Koi should also be offered a higher protein growth food which will encourage healthy streamlined growth. Treat foods may be given occasionally.

The mechanical section of the filter and pre-filter may still require occasional cleaning.

Feed the fish 2-4 times each day on Flake food and Foodsticks including colour enhancing foods. Take care not to overfeed as the water temperature drops. Do not feed regularly below 8°C. Treat foods may be given occasionally.

In a planted pond remove the pump when temperatures drop below 8°C. The pump and filter may then be cleaned. In a fish only pond or if the pump is left running, turn the flow rate to its minimum setting, raise the pump to the water surface and ensure the filter outflow is near the surface to minimise water circulation.

Only feed when the fish are searching for food. Feed once a day on wheatgerm sticks.

TROUBLESHOOTING

PROBLEM	CAUSE	REMEDY
Green water	Suspended algae	Encourage plant growth (particularly oxygenating species). Remove excess debris from pond. Treat with an algicide. If problem persists use a UV sterilising unit.
Hair-like algae on pond side	Blanketweed	As 'Green Water'. The use of a UV unit often encourages blanketweed. Install a vegetable filter to remove excess nutrients.
Water cloudy (Brown water)	Disturbed debris	Remove excess debris from pond. Ensure soil is not washed into pond during heavy rain. Plant all plants in baskets and cover upper surface with gravel.
Fish not feeding	Water Temperature less than 8°C	Stop feeding until fish show interest in food.
	Sudden drop in water temperature	Stop feeding until fish show interest in food.
	Poor water quality	Check water quality and correct.
	Fish unhealthy	Check fish for disease and treat.